THE NO ✈ FUSS GUIDE TO
DUBLIN

THE PRACTICAL, RELATABLE, NO-NONSENSE GUIDE

CONTENTS

YOUR GUIDE TO DUBLIN

How to use this guidebook	6 - 7
Planning your trip	8 - 27
Itineraries	28 - 37
Exploring Dublin	39 - 41

O'CONNELL STREET

Things to see & do	42 - 59
Where to eat & drink	60 - 67
Where to stay	68 - 69

SMITHFIELD & STONEYBATTER

Things to see & do	70 - 83
Where to eat & drink	84 - 89
Where to stay	90 - 91

THE LIBERTIES & KILMAINHAM

Things to see & do	92 - 111
Where to eat & drink	112 - 115
Where to stay	116 - 117

TEMPLE BAR

Things to see & do	118 - 129
Where to eat & drink	130 - 135
Where to stay	136 - 137

GRAFTON STREET, ST STEPHEN'S GREEN & PORTOBELLO

Things to see & do	138 - 157
Where to eat & drink	158 - 167
Where to stay	168 - 169

MERRION SQUARE & FITZWILLIAM SQUARE

Things to see & do	170 - 181
Where to eat & drink	182 - 185
Where to stay	186 - 187

THE DOCKLANDS

Things to see & do	188 - 201
Where to eat & drink	202 - 205
Where to stay	206 - 207

BEYOND THE CITY

Things to see & do	208 - 219
Where to eat & drink	220 - 225
Where to stay	226 - 227
Day Trips from Dublin	228 - 229

ADDITIONAL INFORMATION

Essential Information	230 - 245
Index	248 - 253
Our Story	254 - 259

HOW TO USE
THE DUBLIN GUIDE

Hello! We're **No Fuss Travel Guides.** Our independent guidebooks are crafted with a unique, personal touch, blending thorough research with genuine, first-hand experiences, written in our 'no fuss' style. In this guidebook, you'll discover an insightful exploration of the city's finest offerings—from hidden gems to popular attractions to the best places to eat and stay. All recommendations are unbiased and authentic, as seen through the lens of our dedicated team.

Our mission is to simplify your planning process while making it fun and informative. We strive to equip readers with all the necessary tools to plan and navigate their trips with ease. So, with that being said, below you'll find information on how to make the most of the key features within this guide. Happy travels!

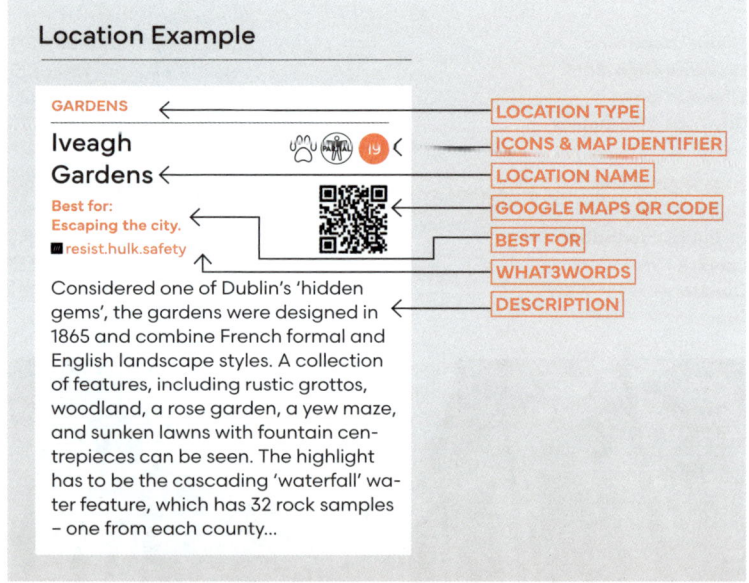

BOOK CARE: DO NOT FLATTEN THE BOOK WHEN OPEN, THIS WILL DAMAGE THE SPINE AND MAY LEAD TO PAGES BECOMING LOOSE. EXTREME HEAT AND DIRECT SUNLIGHT MAY ALSO CAUSE DAMAGE.

FINDING LOCATIONS

The most efficient way of finding locations on your trip is by scanning the QR code next to each location with your smart phone camera. This will open the Google Maps app on your smart phone. Make sure you download this app. Within the app you can also search for a location name, forget using postcodes and full addresses.

The what3words app will pinpoint a location within 3 square metres.

Icon Key

 DOG-FRIENDLY *(RESTRICTIONS MAY APPLY)*

 VEGAN OPTIONS *(WHERE TO EAT PAGES)*

 FULLY ACCESSIBLE

 PARTIALLY ACCESSIBLE

 MAP IDENTIFIER

Accessibility Icons

We've included accessibility information for locations, eateries and accommodation where it is clearly provided by attraction operators. Partial accessibility could mean that part of a building is not accessible or that a hotel only has a small selection of accessible rooms. Always double check ahead of visiting if you have specific accessibility requirements.

GOOGLE MAPS OFFLINE

Downloading Google Maps for offline use before your trip will allow you to still use Google Maps without phone signal. Here's how to do it...

01 | Download and open the Google Maps app on your phone.

02 | Search for the term 'Dublin'.

03 | Scroll across the blue tabs to the right until you find 'Download offline map' and click it.

04 | Zoom in or out to ensure Google downloads all of the area you intend to visit then hit **DOWNLOAD** in the bottom right corner.

05 | Once this downloads, you're good to go!

Planning Your Trip

In this section you'll find everything you need to know about planning an epic trip to Dublin - from detailed itineraries to annual events and expert travel tips!

PAGES 8 - 27

SAY HELLO
TO DUBLIN

Welcome to Dublin—a city bursting with authentic Irish charm! Picture yourself in a cosy Temple Bar pub, the air alive with the sound of traditional music, as you savour a perfectly poured pint of Guinness. But there's far more to this vibrant capital than its world-famous stout. From fascinating history and stunning architecture to buzzing nightlife and cultural gems, Dublin is a city waiting to be explored!

So, if you're not just here for the Guinness, you might be wondering: what makes Dublin such a fantastic destination? Well, it's certainly packed with history and culture, and it boasts a vibrant atmosphere that's simply irresistible! Picture yourself strolling through cobbled streets, marvelling at Dublin Castle or exploring Trinity College to admire the remarkable Book of Kells. With many literary legends calling it home, Dublin is a paradise for book lovers.

Dublin is incredible by day, but after dark? That's when the city really comes to life! Head to Temple Bar, where the streets hum with energy, traditional pubs overflow with live music, and the craic is absolutely unbeatable. Whether you're up for a lively singalong with the locals or just fancy soaking up the warm Irish hospitality, the night is yours to enjoy!

Oh, and whilst you're visiting, be sure to dive into the city's diverse culinary scene—there's something for every taste, from hearty Irish dishes to trendy Michelin-starred restaurants showcasing innovative cuisine.

One of the best things about Dublin? It's an absolute dream to explore on foot! Wander through its character-packed neighbourhoods, from the historic Liberties to the artsy vibes of Smithfield. Need a breather? Head to St. Stephen's Green, a gorgeous park where you can stroll past scenic gardens, unwind by the tranquil lakes, or even pop into a nearby museum. It's the perfect spot for a laid-back afternoon in the heart of the city!

With direct flights from major US cities and just a short hop from the UK and Europe, Dublin is the ultimate last-minute getaway! Whether you're squeezing in a whirlwind weekend or taking your time to soak up more of Ireland's magic, you've made a brilliant choice by visiting the country's capital. So, keep reading to uncover everything you need for an unforgettable trip!

A SNAPSHOT
OF DUBLIN

From the buzzing cobblestone streets of Temple Bar to the stunning campus of Trinity College and the historic Dublin Castle, there's no shortage of amazing spots to explore! While these iconic landmarks are definitely must-sees, Dublin is packed with hidden gems too—think quirky boutiques, trendy cafés, and local art galleries. But don't worry, we've got you covered! To make planning your trip a breeze, we've rounded up the top highlights you simply can't miss in this fantastic city.

01 TRINITY COLLEGE

Step back in time at Trinity College, Ireland's oldest university, founded in 1592 by Queen Elizabeth I. With inspiration from Oxford and Cambridge, it's home to the iconic Old Library, where the famous Book of Kells is kept, and the breathtaking Long Room, packed with over 250,000 rare books!

02 GUINNESS STOREHOUSE

Sip on the ultimate pint of the 'black stuff' at Dublin's Guinness Storehouse! Journey through seven floors of history, brewing secrets, and iconic Guinness culture, culminating in the stunning 360° views of Dublin from the Gravity Bar. No visit to Dublin is complete without visiting this place!

MUST-VISIT MUSEUMS

KILMAINHAM GAOL MUSEUM
PAGE 104

LITTLE MUSEUM OF DUBLIN
PAGE 176

EPIC THE IRISH EMIGRATION MUSEUM
PAGE 192

THE JEANIE JOHNSTON
PAGE 192

TOP TRADITIONAL IRISH PUBS

THE BRAZEN HEAD
PAGE 113

THE TEMPLE BAR
PAGE 123

DARKEY KELLY'S
PAGE 130

THE LONG HALL
PAGE 160

A SNAPSHOT OF DUBLIN

03 ST STEPHEN'S GREEN

Escape the bustle of the city at Dublin's charming Victorian park, St. Stephen's Green. Wander through tree-lined paths, vibrant flowerbeds and past the serene lake. Just around the corner, you'll also find the Museum of Literature – definitely worth a visit while you're in the area!

04 DUBLIN CASTLE

Located in the heart of Dublin, this historic landmark features the stunning State Apartments, the beautiful Chapel Royal, and a 13th-century tower. It's also home to the Chester Beatty Library, a treasure trove of rare manuscripts and art from around the world that are waiting to be explored!

EVERYTHING YOU NEED TO KNOW
ABOUT DUBLIN

Before You Go

To make the most of your Dublin city break, we'd recommend making a rough plan of things you want to do ahead of time. Some spots and experiences book up fast, so here's what we'd suggest doing before you get there.

CHECKLIST:

Up to 2-3 Months Ahead | If you're visiting in summer, it's essential to book your accommodation early. This is also the time to secure tickets for any major concerts or events. Plus, if you're hoping to dine at one of Dublin's Michelin-starred restaurants, you'll need to make those reservations now too.

Up to 3 Weeks Ahead | Travelling off-peak? You can likely book your stay now, along with theatre tickets, reservations for popular weekend spots, and tickets for must-see attractions like Kilmainham Gaol.

Up to 1 Week Ahead | Time to finalise any weekday dining plans at trendy restaurants, and reserve spots for guided tours or major attractions, like the Guinness Storehouse, the Book of Kells, or a whiskey distillery tour.

On Arrival

Thanks to Dublin's compact size and convenient transport options, you can get from your arrival point to the city centre in no time.

ARRIVING:

By Air | Dublin Airport is just 10km from the city centre, making it a quick and easy journey into town. A taxi will get you there in about 30-40 minutes for around €30. For a budget-friendly option, catch an Aircoach bus, they run every 15 minutes directly to the city centre and cost around 10 per person. Alternatively, the Dublin Express offers a direct route along the River Liffey to Heuston Station.

By Ferry | You'll find buses from the port to the city centre running hourly from 7am to 7pm (6pm on Sundays) costing around €2, with a quick 20-minute trip.

By Train | Dublin's two main train stations, Connolly and Heuston, are well connected by the Luas Red Line and several Dublin Bus routes, making it easy to head right into town.

By Bus | The main bus depot, Busáras, is near Connolly Station and serves all Bus Éireann routes, while private coaches generally make stops along the quays.

IMPORTANT TO KNOW

CURRENCY
Euros €

LANGUAGE
English & Irish

EMERGENCY
Call 999 or 112

PAYMENT
Credit cards, debit cards and Apple Pay are accepted in most restaurants, hotels and shops.

VISAS
UK, EEA and US citizens do not require a visa when travelling to Dublin for tourism or business stays.

MOBILE PHONES
All European, US and Australasian phones work in Dublin, though it's a good idea to check with your provider. You can also purchase SIM cards locally and eSIMs online.

TOURIST INFORMATION CENTRES
Barnardo Square | 3 Palace Street, D02 T277. O'Connell Street | 14 Upper O'Connell Street, D01 WP59.

USEFUL APPS TO DOWNLOAD

GOOGLE MAPS
FOR LOCATIONS & DIRECTIONS

TFI LEAP TOP-UP
A PREPAID TRAVEL CARD

TFI LIVE
FOR TRAVEL UPDATES

BOLT
FOR BOOKING A TAXI

FREE NOW
FOR BOOKING A TAXI

DUBLIN BIKES
FOR CITY BIKE RENTAL

REVOLUT
FOR CONVERTING CURRENCY

HANDY WEBSITES TO KNOW ABOUT

DO DUBLIN
FOR DAYS OUT PASSES & TICKETS

GO CITY
FOR DAYS OUT PASSES & TICKETS

DISCOVER IRELAND
FOR THE BEST THINGS TO SEE & DO

LOVIN DUBLIN
FOR NEWS, EATERIES & EVENTS

DUBLIN TOWN
FOR NEWS, EATERIES & EVENTS

TRIP ADVISOR
HOTEL & RESTAURANT REVIEWS

ALL THE FOOD
RESTAURANT RECOMMENDATIONS

Getting Around

TRANSPORT LINKS:

Bus | The bus network serves both the city and its suburbs, with most routes running from 5am to midnight. If you're using a Leap card, bus prices are standardised so simply tap your card when you board, and you're good to go. If you're paying cash, make sure you have the exact change for your ticket.

DART | The Dublin Area Rapid Transit (DART) trains are perfect for reaching the city centre and coastline. You can grab a ticket at any station or use a Leap card for convenience.

Luas | Dublin's tram service has two main lines: the red line, which runs east-west across the Northside, and the green line, running north-south. Tickets are available at every station, or you can use a Leap card.

Bike | You can use Dublin bikes to cycle around the city, we'd suggest downloading the app for ease.

Accessibility

Dublin is fairly accessible, with many key attractions being fully or partially accessible. You can also find hotel rooms catering to those with disabilities around the city.

For more information on Accessible travel head to page 232.

USEFUL INFORMATION:

Please Offer Me A Seat | For those who may have an invisible disability, you can request a 'Please Offer Me a Seat' badge and card at bus and rail stations throughout Dublin.

Travel Assistance Scheme | For anyone with a disability or reduced mobility, this scheme offers a travel assistant who can join you on your first few journeys, and provide useful advice on planning your trips.

REFER TO PAGES 230 - 245 FOR MORE ESSENTIAL INFORMATION

EVERYTHING YOU NEED TO KNOW
ABOUT DUBLIN

Dublin Tours

If it's your first time in Dublin, navigating the city might be easier with a guided tour or a hop-on-hop-off bus. There are plenty of options to choose from, and the below are just a few that could be helpful if you're planning to visit multiple attractions around the city.

OTHER WAYS TO SEE THE CITY:

DoDublin Bus Tour | A convenient way to explore the city, with flexible 24 hour or 48 hour tickets, as well as a freedom pass that allows you to use the full Dublin bus network for 72 hours. Operating daily from 9am, the last tour runs at 7pm in summer and 5pm in winter, with buses usually around every 20 minutes, offering plenty of time to see Dublin's top sights at your own pace.

Dublin Big Bus Hop-on Hop-off Tour | They also offer 24 hour and 48 hour tickets, including the Explore Ticket which includes a half day tour to the coastal village of Howth. Tours begin at Stop #1 on Upper O'Connell Street, with hop-on, hop-off access at any stop from 9am to 5pm, or later for night tours.

Cycle Dublin Bike Tour | A unique and eco-friendly way to see most of Dublin in just two and a half hours. Tours are at 10.30am and 2pm 7-days a week, you can also get electric bikes for an additional fee.

Dublin Discovered Boat Tour | Explore Dublin's landmarks by boat. This 45-minute guided tour departs daily from the Sean O'Casey Footbridge, offering a unique view of the city with live commentary from expert guides.

Dublin Passes

If you're looking to visit several attractions in Dublin, it might be worth considering a pass that gives you access to multiple sites at a discounted rate.

ATTRACTION PASSES:

Go City Dublin Explorer Pass | A flexible and cost-effective way to explore, this pass allows you to access attractions of your choice and is valid for 60 days from the first visit. You can choose the attractions as you go, although it's worth booking popular ones in advance. Download the Go City app and scan at each location for entry, saving both time and money compared to standard ticket prices.

Go City All Inclusive Pass | This pass gives access to as many attractions as you can fit in, making it ideal if you're wanting to see and do more. You can choose a pass duration of 1 to 5 days, and save on price compared to individual tickets - perfect for a jam packed itinerary!

DoDublin Days Out Card | With this card you can explore six of Dublin's top attractions and save 25% compared to individual tickets, and can use it anytime within 12 months. You may also want to upgrade to the Days Out Card Plus to include a Hop-on Hop-off tour.

DoDublin Freedom Ticket | An all-in-one pass for getting around Dublin. It offers unlimited access to buses, trams (Luas), and trains (DART), plus airport routes and 48 hours on the city's top Hop-on Hop-off tour. With 72 hours of travel, it's great for a short city stay.

GET YOUR GO CITY PASS

WHAT IS THE GO CITY PASS?
A sight-seeing pass, that gives you access to must-see attractions, including the Guinness Storehouse, Dublin Castle, Jameson Distillery and more at a discounted price.

SO, HOW DOES IT WORK?
1. Buy your pass online
2. Receive your pass as a barcode
3. Scan yourself straight into attractions and save €€!

some attractions require pre-booking using your booking number.

WHAT ARE THE PASS OPTIONS?

Explorer Pass: Allows access to your chosen number of attractions. Choose between 3 - 7 attractions.

All Inclusive Pass: Gives you access to as many attractions as you can fit in. Choose between 1 - 5 days.

WHAT WILL I SAVE?
If you chose the 'All Inclusive Pass', for 2 days at a cost of €109 and followed the itinerary below you would save €99!

DAY 1:	USUAL ENTRY PRICE:
Big Bus Hop-on Hop-off	€35 (24-hour ticket)
Dublin Castle	€8
Dublinia Viking Museum	€14
Teeling Whiskey Distillery	€20
Guinness Storehouse	€30 (weekend entry price)

DAY 2:	USUAL ENTRY PRICE:
GPO Museum	€17
National Wax Museum Plus	€19
Irish Rock N' Roll Museum	€26
EPIC Museum	€23
Jeanie Johnston	€16

SCAN THE QR CODE
TO GET YOUR GO CITY PASS
& SAVE ON TOP ATTRACTIONS

MUSEUMS | EXPERIENCES | TOURS | LANDMARKS

FIRST-TIME TRAVEL TIPS
FOR DUBLIN

Where To Stay

Dublin has no shortage of places to stay, whatever your budget. If you're after luxury head to the St. Stephen's Green area or the charming Merrion Square & Fitzwilliam Square district, where you'll find upscale 5-star hotels. Alternatively, for budget-friendly finds, Temple Bar has many affordable hostels and hotel options to choose from.

If you want a taste of local life, consider staying in Portobello, Smithfield or Stoneybatter. These trendy neighbourhoods also have a range of cool bars, cafés and eateries.

What To Pack

Dublin is generally casual, so opt for comfortable clothing unless you're heading to glamorous events or fine dining spots. Since the weather can be unpredictable, it's best to pack layers and a waterproof jacket.

CHECKLIST:

- [ ] Raincoat
- [ ] Umbrella
- [ ] Transitional Layers
- [ ] Comfortable Walking Shoes
- [ ] Easily Accessible Day Bag
- [ ] Plug Adapter (3 Prong Outlet)
- [ ] No Fuss Travel Dublin City Guide
- [ ] Euros

Where To Eat

Dublin's food scene offers everything, from budget bites to fine dining!

For a trendy spot, head to Manor Street in Stoneybatter, where you'll find Italian favourites at Grano and crispy fried chicken at Korean Table. If fine dining is more your style, The Liberties district has a range of upscale eateries such as Etto and Hugo's, where you'll be able to sample expertly crafted dishes. After something a little more casual? Take a stroll down Capel Street for some of the city's best Asian eats, from sushi to ramen and bánh mì!

Local Etiquette

Typically, tipping in restaurants isn't required; however, if you receive good service, it's considered polite to leave a tip of 10% to 20%. Some restaurants may also add a service charge to your bill, and if this is included, there's no need to tip.

If someone buys drinks for you and your mates, it's probably part of a "round." The idea is to take turns buying, so everyone gets a chance to treat the group and keep it fair!

Dubliners like to queue and aren't fans of anyone skipping the line. They're also known for saying "sorry" quite a bit, even in place of "excuse me".

BUDGET BREAKDOWN
COSTS IN DUBLIN

Accommodation

Now, depending on how luxurious you want your stay to be, hotel prices vary considerably. Luckily there's plenty of hotel options to choose from for varying budgets.

AVERAGE COST:

Based on one standard double room:

Budget-friendly Hotel | Typically this would cost around €100 - €160 per night.

Mid-range Hotel | If you're after a bit more comfort and style, expect to pay around €190–€230 a night.

Premium Hotel | For those looking to indulge in a luxurious 5-star stay, rates are between €250 - €300+ per night.

Food & Drink

If you're a foodie, be ready to budget for everything from affordable pizza slices and street food bites to the splurge-worthy delights of Michelin-starred restaurants. Prices can range from a few euros to a few hundred!

AVERAGE COST:

Pint of Guinness | €9.95 at Temple Bar vs. €5 in local budget-friendly spots.

Coffee & Cake | Treat yourself to a coffee and a slice of cake for €6–€10.

Brunch | Expect to pay around €12–€18 for a hearty brunch at trendy cafés, with more upscale spots reaching €20+.

Fine Dining Meal | A gourmet meal at a fine dining restaurant will typically set you back €70–€120+ per person.

Transport

When using transport around Dublin, Bus and Luas tickets provide great value and convenient access throughout the city. Taxis however, are understandably more expensive.

AVERAGE COST:

Bus Ticket | A bus ticket fare to go a short distance costs around €3 per trip.

Air Coach | Travelling from Dublin airport to the city centre will cost €10 per person one-way.

Luas | For a 90-minute fare the Luas costs just around €2.

Taxi | A 30-40 minute taxi from the airport to the city will cost around €30.

Attractions

Many top attractions, like museums and galleries, offer free entry or have a small fee. However, popular spots like the Guinness Storehouse or Dublin Castle are slightly more expensive.

AVERAGE COST:

Trinity College | Adult entry is €33.50, including a 45-minute guided tour, the Long Room, and the Book of Kells.

Dublin Castle | Adult entry is €8.00.

Kilmainham Gaol | Adult tickets are €8. For this you'll also get access to a guided tour around the historic prison.

Guinness Storehouse | Entry costs begin at €20 per adult, which includes a complimentary pint of Guinness.

FREE MUSEUMS & GALLERIES

HUGH LANE GALLERY
PAGE 49

NATIONAL MUSEUM OF IRELAND - DECORATIVE ARTS | PAGE 78

IRISH MUSEUM OF MODERN ART
PAGE 104

PHOTO MUSEUM IRELAND
PAGE 124

CHESTER BEATTY
PAGE 146

NATIONAL MUSEUM OF IRELAND - ARCHAEOLOGY | PAGE 175

NATIONAL MUSEUM OF IRELAND - NATURAL HISTORY | PAGE 175

ADDITIONAL FREE ATTRACTIONS

NATIONAL BOTANIC GARDENS
PAGE 55

PHOENIX PARK
PAGE 78

DUBLIN CASTLE GROUNDS
PAGE 146

ST STEPHEN'S GREEN
PAGE 150

NATIONAL LIBRARY OF IRELAND
PAGE 174

MERRION SQUARE PARK
PAGE 175

GRAND CANAL DOCK
PAGE 196

FIRST-TIME TRAVEL TIPS

DAILY BUDGET BREAKDOWN

WHAT WE SPENT IN A DAY (PER PERSON)
DAY 1
Food & Drink: €36
Transport: €0 (walking)
Attractions: €18
Accommodation: €80

WHAT WE SPENT IN A DAY (PER PERSON)
DAY 2
Food & Drink: €38
Transport: €14 (bus & uber)
Attractions: €27
Accommodation: €80

WHAT WE SPENT IN A DAY (PER PERSON)
DAY 3
Food & Drink: €47
Transport: €16 (bus & uber)
Attractions: €29.50
Accommodation: €80

WHAT WE SPENT IN A DAY (PER PERSON)
DAY 4
Food & Drink: €36
Transport: €8 (tram)
Attractions: €32
Accommodation: €80

BEST FOOD SPOTS
IN DUBLIN

While food might not be the first thing that comes to mind when thinking of Dublin, trust us when we say the city has some excellent and delicious dining options. From Michelin-starred restaurants to street food and traditional Irish dishes, Dublin offers a vibrant mix of cuisines - Italian, French, Korean, Spanish, and of course, Irish. Whether you're seeking a fine dining experience or a casual quick bite, you certainly won't go hungry. To help you out, we've rounded up the best foodie spots and streets you need to try - be warned, you might just need to extend your stay!

01 CAPEL STREET

A vibrant hub of culture and cuisine, offering diverse foodie spots like Brother Hubbard (North) for brunch, Musashi for sushi and noodles, Dash Burger for indulgent smash burgers, and Krewe North for a taste of New Orleans. Also, for delicious Korean BBQ, Arisu is a must-visit!

02 CAMDEN STREET

Named among the 'coolest' streets in the world by Time Out magazine, it's no surprise this area has an incredible line-up of restaurants. From the bold Indian flavours at Pickle, and the wood-fired cuisine at Mister S, to the fusion dishes at Hang Dai, there's sure to be something here for everyone!

NO FUSS FOODIE FAVOURITES

BREAKFAST: TWO PUPS
PAGE 115

BRUNCH: TANG
PAGE 164

LUNCH: MANI
PAGE 159

DINNER: NUTBUTTER
PAGE 85

FINE DINING & BEST RATED FOOD SPOTS

CHAPTER ONE
MODERN FRENCH CUISINE, PAGE 61

MR FOX
MODERN EUROPEAN CUISINE, PAGE 62

MATSUKAWA
JAPANESE CUISINE, PAGE 84

VARIETY JONES
FAMILY-STYLE MODERN CUISINE, PAGE 113

D'OLIER STREET
MODERN CUISINE, PAGE 133

PICHET
FRENCH CUISINE, PAGE 158

KICKY'S
MEDITERRANEAN CUISINE, PAGE 159

UNO MAS
MEDITERRANEAN CUISINE, PAGE 160

GLOVERS ALLEY
MODERN CUISINE, PAGE 164

BIGFAN
ASIAN CUISINE, PAGE 164

LA GORDITA
SPANISH CUISINE, PAGE 164

MISTER S
MODERN CUISINE, PAGE 166

ETTO
MODERN EUROPEAN CUISINE, PAGE 182

OSTERIA LUCO
ITALIAN CUISINE, PAGE 204

03 MANOR STREET

Another trendy spot is Manor Street in Stoneybatter, home to cool cafés including Social Fabric and Joli. Dining options include Grano, known for its authentic Italian dishes, L. Mulligan Grocer for hearty gastropub eats, and Vietnom for (the clue's in the name) traditional Vietnamese bites.

04 DRURY STREET

Just a few streets away from Grafton Street, Dublin's vibrant Creative Quarter, is a foodie's paradise. Here, you'll find spots like Amy Austin, known for its wine and small plates, MASA for Mexican, and Bambino Pizza for moreish slices. Fade Street Social is also a good option for a tipple or two.

MONTHLY GUIDE
TO DUBLIN

January

Dublin's weather this time of year tends to be cold and rainy, so make sure you layer up and prepare for the chill. But don't let that put you off – it's the ideal season to cosy up in pubs and dive into the city's lively cultural scene!

KEY EVENTS

New Year Celebrations | Kick off the year with the lively energy of Dublin's famous pubs, and what better way to welcome the New Year than with a pint of Guinness in hand?

Tradfest | Every January, this bustling festival lights up Dublin with the very best in Irish music, featuring top talent from both established and emerging artists!

February

February is the off-season in Dublin, offering a chance to explore the city's attractions with fewer crowds. While the weather may be chilly and rainy, it's also a perfect time to find great deals on flights and hotels!

KEY EVENTS

Dublin International Film Festival | Each February, Dublin showcases a fantastic line-up of Irish and international films, that celebrate the art of world-class film making!

Six Nations Rugby | A must for sports fans! The season runs from February to April, bringing electrifying matches and a lively atmosphere to Dublin's Aviva Stadium.

March

March is a bustling month, with St. Patrick's Day marking the busiest weekend of the year as visitors come from far and wide. While the weather can be rainy, the lively atmosphere makes it a great time to visit.

KEY EVENTS

St. Patrick's Day | Get ready for a global celebration of Irish arts, culture, and heritage, featuring the legendary St. Patrick's Day Parade. Join the festivities as Dublin comes alive with vibrant music, dancing, and Irish pride, with crowds lining the streets. If you're in town around March 17th, it's an experience you definitely won't want to miss out on!

> SUMMER, ESPECIALLY JULY AND AUGUST, IS PRICIER DUE TO THE HOLIDAY SEASON, SO IT'S BEST TO PLAN AND BOOK AHEAD.

April

April typically brings milder weather, though showers are highly likely. With the Easter holidays usually falling in this month, it can be busier, so it's worth checking as hotel prices tend to rise during this period.

KEY EVENTS

Irish Grand National | A thrilling horse racing event held at Fairyhouse Racecourse, that brings together top tier competitors and racing fans from all over. It's a must-see on Ireland's sporting calendar!

May

May brings milder weather, making it the perfect time to explore the city and check out outdoor festivals! Plus, the early May Bank Holiday means many locals enjoy an extended weekend so the city really comes alive.

KEY EVENTS

Dublin Literature Festival | An annual celebration of books and storytelling that unites writers, poets, and creatives from around the world for readings, interviews, and workshops.

Bord Bia Bloom | Held in Phoenix Park at the end of May, the event features stunning show gardens, food markets, cooking demonstrations, and a range of family-friendly activities.

Dublin Dance Festival | Each May DDF showcases top Irish and international dance performances held in a range of venues across the city.

June

The warmer weather is perfect for discovering all that the city has to offer. Just keep in mind that festivals and events can make things a bit livelier, leading to busier streets and some price hikes on hotels.

KEY EVENTS

Dublin Pride | This epic annual event is the biggest of its kind in Ireland, shining a rainbow spotlight on the city's diverse LGBTQIA+ community. With a series of exciting events leading up to the grand finale, a spectacular pride parade on the last Saturday of June.

Forbidden Fruit Festival | Taking place in the heart of Dublin at the stunning Museum of Modern Art, this vibrant festival showcases a diverse line-up of alternative music acts.

MONTHLY GUIDE
TO DUBLIN

July

July brings better weather with long, sunny days ideal for exploring the city's attractions. However, it can get busy with schools and colleges on break, resulting in lively crowds and higher hotel prices.

KEY EVENTS

Trinity Summer Series | A stand-out on Ireland's gig calendar, Trinity Summer Series showcases top musical talent in a stunning outdoor setting at Trinity College, perfect for music lovers!

Longitude Festival | A popular summer music event showcasing local and international artists across genres including pop, hip-hop, and electro, drawing in music fans from all over.

City Spectacular | Enjoy two days of free street performances at Merrion Square - think acrobats, sword swallowers and magicians! Don't forget to toss a coin or two into their hats!

August

In August, the summer holidays continue in Dublin, bringing even more visitors to the city. Enjoy warm weather and a vibrant atmosphere, with plenty of outdoor events.

KEY EVENTS

Dublin Horse Show | A prestigious equestrian event held since 1864, showcases the best in horse riding and jumping. But it's not just about the horses, join Ladies Day for contests and awards celebrating the best dressed!

September

After the summer peak, September is a slightly quieter time to visit Dublin. It's perfect for enjoying all there is to see in the city without the crowds, while still experiencing vibrant events like the Dublin Fringe Festival.

KEY EVENTS

Dublin Fringe Festival | A lively celebration of arts and culture, featuring innovative performances in theatre, dance, comedy, and more. Held across the city in September, it's a must-visit for anyone looking to experience Dublin's vibrant creative scene.

Dublin Culture Night | Discover the city's hidden gems after hours! This exciting event offers free access to galleries, museums, theatres, and cultural institutions, allowing visitors to explore and enjoy a variety of performances, and exhibitions for one night only.

> **WITH DUBLIN'S UNPREDICTABLE WEATHER, LAYERING UP IS THE WAY TO GO – BE READY FOR WHATEVER THE DAY THROWS AT YOU!**

October

As you've probably guessed, Dublin's weather is notoriously unpredictable, with anything from mild days to cold spells. As it's shoulder season, flights tend to be cheaper, and crowds are fewer, making it a great time to visit.

KEY EVENTS

Bram Stoker Festival | A thrilling celebration that honours the legendary author of Dracula! Held over Halloween weekend, it's packed with spooky film screenings, haunting performances, and spine-chilling storytelling.
Dublin Theatre Festival | Running from late September to early October, this event shows off the city's vibrant performing arts scene held in various venues throughout the city.
Dublin Marathon | Held annually, the marathon winds through the heart of the city, showcasing Dublin's landmarks and bustling neighbourhoods.

November

November is a quieter time to visit with fewer tourists also making it more affordable. The weather can be wet and relatively cold so be sure to wrap up with layers and a rain jacket!

KEY EVENTS

Dublin Book Festival | The festival features a fantastic line-up of authors, poets, and events - a great time to visit if you're a book lover! With engaging book readings, lively panel discussions, and fun workshops.

December

Christmas in Dublin is pure magic! Think festive markets and fairy lights, perfect for a leisurely stroll. Just keep in mind flights and hotel prices can soar during the Christmas period, so plan ahead if you're on a budget!

KEY EVENTS

Dublin Castle Christmas Market | Usually held in the historic courtyard of Dublin Castle, the market is filled with twinkling lights, festive decor, and over 30 traditional wooden chalets. Be sure to check dates and times as this can vary year to year.
Leopards Town Races | This traditional annual event combines horse racing with festive cheer. Off the track, visitors can enjoy live music, seasonal treats, and a lively festive atmosphere.

Itineraries

On the following pages you'll find some suggested itineraries that may help your planning, depending on the amount of time you have in Dublin and the type of trip you're looking for - from one day in Dublin to a local's guide.

PAGES 28 - 37

ONE DAY ONLY
IN DUBLIN

01 A WHISTLE-STOP TOUR TO ALL THE BEST BITS

9:00 AM | After having a quick bite to eat and coffee to fuel your morning, jump on the **Big Bus Hop-on Hop-off Tour** (included with a Go City Pass) to take you around Dublin's top attractions. It's the perfect way to see more of the city.

10:00 AM | Hop off at **Trinity College**, steeped in centuries of academic tradition you can explore its historic and picturesque grounds, a peaceful escape in the heart of the city. Take a look around the magnificent **Long Room Library** and the **Book of Kells**, a beautifully illuminated manuscript.

12:00 PM | Next, head to **Dublin Castle** where you can explore underground tunnels, the Chapel Royal and it's Medieval Tower. If the weather allows you can also take a stroll around the gardens.

1:00 PM | Located within the Dublin Castle complex, **Chester Beatty Library** is also worth taking a look at, showcasing manuscripts, rare books, and artistic artefacts from around the world.

2:00 PM | Stop by **Beanhive**, a cosy café known for its generously filled sandwiches. Whether you're craving something savoury, a sweet treat, or a quick caffeine fix, their menu options are sure to hit the spot.

3:00 PM | Take a leisurely walk along **Grafton Street**, Dublin's prime shopping district. Browse the boutiques, street performers, and iconic stores.

4:00 PM | Make your way to the **Guinness Storehouse**, arguably Dublin's most famous attraction. Learn about the history of Ireland's iconic stout and enjoy a perfectly poured pint at the Gravity Bar, with panoramic views of the city.

6:00 PM | Make a quick stop at the **Ha'penny Bridge**, the first pedestrian bridge to span the River Liffey and used to cost ha'penny to cross (hence the name Ha'penny Bridge).

6:30 PM | No trip to Dublin is complete without a visit to the iconic **Temple Bar Pub**, famous for its lively atmosphere. The area is also a great place to enjoy traditional Irish music, before heading back home.

A WEEKEND
IN DUBLIN

01 DAY ONE | FROM MUSEUMS TO MUSIC

Morning | Head straight to **Ebb & Flow Camden** for a delicious breakfast and coffee to start your day off right. From here, head to the **Museum of Literature Ireland (MoLI)** to dive into Dublin's literary heritage. After your visit, take a leisurely stroll through the tranquil **St. Stephen's Green** before continuing to the **National Museum of Archaeology**.

Afternoon | After a morning of museums, you'll be getting peckish, so head to **The Bank on College Green** for a gourmet sandwich. While you're nearby, snap a quick photo with the iconic **Molly Malone statue** before making your way to the **Temple Bar Gallery and Studios**.

Evening | Now it's time to soak up the lively atmosphere of the **Temple Bar** district. Join a **Musical Pub Crawl** with live Irish music and storytelling led by local musicians.

02 DAY TWO | EXPERIENCE THE LOCAL HOTSPOTS

Morning | Start your day with a hearty breakfast at **Brother Hubbard North**. Then, explore Ireland's revolutionary past at the **GPO Museum,** you'll need an hour or so here. Next up, pay a visit to **Dublin Castle** and the **Chester Beatty Library**.

Afternoon | After stopping for a treat at **Il Valentino Bakery & Café,** take in the Gothic beauty of **St. Patrick's Cathedral** and its grounds, then make your way over to the **Guinness Storehouse**. There, you can enjoy a fine pint of the black stuff and learn the art of pouring a perfect pint yourself.

Evening | If time allows, try catching a theatre performance at the historic **Gaiety Theatre,** or if you're after something a little more unique you could try the evening **Gravedigger Ghost Bus Tour**.

ITINERARIES

FRIENDS & FOODIE WEEKEND
IN DUBLIN

01 DAY ONE | GETTING TO KNOW DUBLIN

Morning | If there's one thing you should visit in Dublin (other than the Guinness Storehouse) it has to be **Trinity College** to see the Book of Kells, and the stunning Long Room Library. From here, head to the **Little Museum of Dublin** to discover more about the city's history before enjoying a relaxing stroll through **St. Stephen's Green.**

Afternoon | If you're pushed for time grab yourself a quick pizza slice from **Bambino**, or head to **Tang** for healthier options. After lunch, book onto a group **Viking Splash Tour** and yes, you'll have to wear a Viking helmet, it's all part of the fun! After that, dive into Dublin's literary scene with a **Literary Pub Crawl** where you can sip a pint in the same spots as legends like James Joyce and Oscar Wilde.

Evening | For dinner, grab a bite from award winning Chinese restaurant **BIGFAN**, and bag yourself a Wagu cheeseburger. If that doesn't tickle your fancy, there's a few other spots like **Chimac Aungier St, Masa** and **Uno Mas** nearby. Then head for a pint at the gorgeous **Long Hall Pub** before finishing your night with live music at **Devitt's.**

02 DAY TWO | DELVING INTO DUBLIN'S HISTORY

Morning | For breakfast head to the much loved **As One** serving fresh, seasonal goodness. Then, hop on a **Dublin Discovered Boat Tour** and cruise along the River Liffey, soaking in the city's sights. From here, take time for a fun activity, try kayaking with **Surfdock Watersports**. Or, if you and your friends aren't the outdoorsy type, book a group escape room aboard a boat at the aptly named Escape Boats! Have extra time to spare? Visit the **EPIC Museum!**

Afternoon | After all that activity, you'll be ready for a hearty meal. Join the **Secret Food Tour Dublin** and try some of the best traditional Irish dishes. From comforting stews to sweet treats, this three-hour food adventure will keep you fuelled for the day. Once you're happily stuffed, head over to the iconic **Guinness Storehouse** to explore the brewing history and enjoy a perfectly poured pint and 360 views across Dublin.

Evening | End your day in true Dublin style with a **Temple Bar Musical Pub Crawl.** Had enough of the pubs? Head to the **Craic Den Comedy Club** instead, where you can sit back, and enjoy a night of laughs with some of Ireland's funniest comedians.

A THREE DAY LOCAL GUIDE
TO DUBLIN

01 DAY ONE | DELVING INTO THE PAST

Morning | Dublin's proud and chequered past still plays heavily into its present, and a good way to begin to understand the ethos of the place - creativity, individuality, cultural pride - is to make an effort to connect with that history. The **National Museum of Ireland** hosts Ireland's oldest bits, from the creepy still-preserved "bog bodies", pulled from the peat leathery and semi-intact after thousands of years, to ancient, edible butter and reconstructed fairy forts. With the added benefit of overlooking the Irish parliament, **The Dáil**, it's a great place to get historical bearings.

Afternoon | Quick and affordable **Tang** on Dorset Street serves zesty Middle Eastern wraps perfect for lunch walking around gorgeous Guinness family heirloom **St Stephen's Green**, just over the road. Then, the Hogwarts-like **Trinity College Library** and its priceless biblical text the **Book of Kells** offer a stunning glance at the devotional side of Ireland's past.

Evening | For the evening, a glance at the Dublin of old can be found in sampling the city's unique boiled sausage stew, coddle, doubling up with some tunes at boisterously musical **Quay's Bar.**

02 DAY TWO | A LOCAL ANGLE ON THE TOURIST SPOTS

Morning | Don't let cynical locals tell you Temple Bar's not worth a look. The boutique stores show a crafty side of the city, with **Jam Art**, a sales hub for local artists, and the Saturday-only **Temple Bar Food Market** the highlights. While The Temple Bar itself is best saved for an Instagram-moment, the quirky **Irish Film Institute**, heavily left-leaning Connolly Books, and several outdoor pieces of politically significant work by local street-art star Maser add colour.

Afternoon | Dublin's grá for Guinness and whiskey runs deep. **The Open Gate**, tacked on the side of the **Guinness Storehouse**, hosts globally exclusive experimental brews. The Storehouse has the city's best views and, whilst also a tourist trap, has a stark and memorable history. For whiskey lovers, **Teelings** engaging tours will teach you about the Angel's Share.

Evening | Drop in on steak paradise **FX Buckley,** and then explore the real local night-life: locals prefer the area around Aungier Street. For a classic Irish bar, try **The Long Hall** or hit up iconic indie venue **Whelan's** for long nights of live music, pints and dancing.

03 DAY THREE | THE ROAD LESS TRAVELLED

Morning | At Europe's largest urban park, **Phoenix Park**, hire a tandem at the entrance, search out the massive deer population, then hit up the charming **Farmleigh Estate** and its markets, before heading to Europe's longest pub, **The Hole In The Wall**, for a beef and Guinness stew.

Afternoon | Back in the city, beautiful **Marsh's Library** is the kind of musty aside that might require you to clear your lungs with a walk through the seriously underrated **Liberties** district, a once tax-free area outside the city walls now known for antiques and small traders. Hippie-chic **Two Pups** have the best accompanying coffee. If you've time, **Dublin Castle**, en route back towards the city, can make a nice aside: the upstairs rooms are regal and the courtyard, with its gas-lit lamps, feels nostalgic. The best bit, though, is the bowels of the place, where water still trickles through the silt around the old city walls, though you'll need to take a tour to see it.

Evening | The wild mix of cuisine on offer along rugged **Parnell Street** and a stop in the often locally, literary-focused **Gate Theatre** offer a quiet but enticing finale to a long-weekend of Dublin's best.

JAMES HENDICOTT

Meet Dublin local, James Hendicott. James is an exceptionally talented copywriter who started his career in travel writing after accepting a position teaching English in Seoul, South Korea. Since then, he has thrived, creating content for various organisations and developing a unique writing style that reflects his experiences and insights.

James has carefully curated this three-day itinerary, which includes a mix of well-known attractions and lesser-known hidden gems, showcasing a unique perspective that only a local could provide.

FOUR FULL DAYS
IN DUBLIN

01 DAY ONE | GETTING TO KNOW DUBLIN

Morning | Start your day at **Trinity College** to see the Book of Kells and the stunning Long Room Library. Then, head to the **National Museum of Archaeology** to learn about Ireland's history before enjoying a relaxing stroll through **St. Stephen's Green**.

Afternoon | Unwind with afternoon tea on a **Vintage Tea Trips** bus, enjoying scones as you tour the city, or grab a bite to eat from **Tang (Dawson Street).** Afterwards, dive into Irish literary history at the **Museum of Literature Ireland (MoLI),** then wrap up the afternoon exploring the historic halls and grounds of **Dublin Castle**.

Evening | Catch a show at the **Gaiety Theatre,** or dive into the lively atmosphere at one of Grafton Street's pubs. For live music, we recommend **Devitt's,** alternatively **Kehoe's** is a great option.

02 DAY TWO | DELVING INTO DUBLIN'S HISTORY

Morning | Begin your day at **Kilmainham Gaol,** where you can learn about Ireland's history and its fight for independence, along with a tour of the prison. Then, visit the **Irish Museum of Modern Art** to explore contemporary artworks.

Afternoon | Head to the iconic **Guinness Storehouse** for a bite at one of its eateries and a behind-the-scenes look at Ireland's famous stout, complete with a tasting and panoramic views from the Gravity Bar. Afterwards, continue the party by heading to the **Temple Bar** district. Here you can visit the iconic **Temple Bar Gallery and Studios.**

Evening | While in the area, dine at a traditional Dublin pub for local dishes, or try **Pichet** if you're after something a little more upscale. Even better, you could book a **Temple Bar Pub Crawl!**

A WELL-ROUNDED EXPERIENCE, PERFECT FOR FIRST-TIME VISITORS WANTING TO SEE ALL OF THE MUST-SEE SPOTS IN DUBLIN.

03 DAY THREE | A DIFFERENT VIEW OF THE CITY

Morning | Start at the **EPIC Museum** to explore Ireland's emigration history. Then, enjoy a stroll to **Poolbeg Lighthouse,** or if you'd prefer to rest your feet, take a **Dublin Discovered Boat Tour.** For lunch, we recommend heading to **Nut Butter** at the Grand Canal Dock. After lunch, music fans should check out **Windmill Lane Studios!**

Afternoon | Next, head to the O'Connell Street district, where sports fans can explore **Croke Park Stadium and Museum,** also if you're not afraid of heights, try the **Skywalk** for stunning views! Finish the afternoon with a visit to **Hugh Lane Gallery,** followed by **14 Henrietta Street** (pre-book a tour beforehand).

Evening | For dinner, make your way over to **Merrion Square and Fitzwilliam Square** district for a fine dining experience at **Etto** or **Hugo's.**

04 DAY FOUR | EXPERIENCE THE LOCAL HOTSPOTS

Morning | Take some time to explore **Phoenix Park,** and if you're an animal lover, don't miss **Dublin Zoo!** When you're finished roaming the park, pop to the nearby **National Museum of Ireland – Decorative Arts** to take a look at some fascinating exhibits.

Afternoon | Next-up the **Jameson Distillery,** where you can grab lunch nearby at **Mad Yolks,** just a 3-minute walk away. Enjoy a taste of Irish whiskey (if you're not nursing a hangover from the night before). Then, dive into Dublin's past with a **Dublinia Viking Tour** to experience the city's medieval history.

Evening | Wrap up your day in Stoneybatter, one of Dublin's most trendy neighbourhoods. **Grano, L.Mulligan Grocer** and **Fidelity Bar** are worth trying for dinner and drinks.

Exploring Dublin

PAGES 38 - 41

NEIGHBOURHOODS
IN DUBLIN

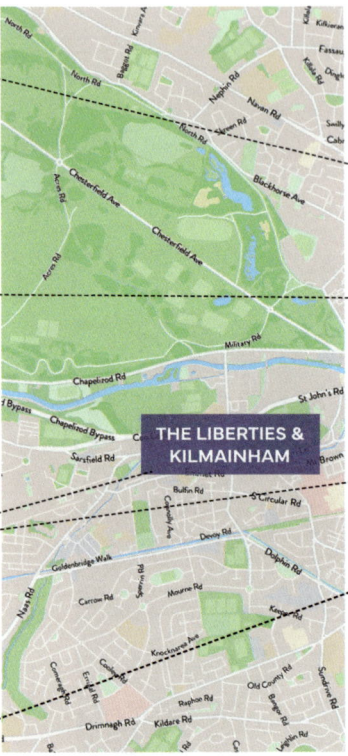

01 O'CONNELL STREET

One of Dublin's busiest and liveliest streets, it's a hub for some of the city's best food spots. Centrally located, with plenty of nearby museums, theatres and bars there's no shortage of things to explore!

02 SMITHFIELD & STONEYBATTER

Smithfield and Stoneybatter are among Dublin's trendiest and most contemporary hangouts, known for their independent cafés, Irish pubs, and top-tier restaurants. You'll also find some key attractions in the area.

03 THE LIBERTIES & KILMAINHAM

Love a good tipple? This is the spot! The birthplace of Guinness and home to distilleries like Roe & Co and Pearse Lyons, it has plenty to offer. It also has historic landmarks such as Kilmainham Gaol and Marsh's Library.

04 TEMPLE BAR

Dublin's most iconic spot, Temple Bar, is brimming with lively pubs, eateries, and boutiques. It's a must-visit to soak up the fun atmosphere, with plenty of hotel options nearby, it's perfect for a short stay in the city.

05 GRAFTON STREET & ST STEPHEN'S GREEN

St. Stephen's Green is perfect for a leisurely stroll, whilst Grafton Street is full of shops, cafés, eateries and street performers. With so many must-see spots and hotels nearby, it's a great place to explore and stay.

SCAN THE QR CODE TO ACCESS OUR DUBLIN GOOGLE MAP, ALLOWING YOU TO EASILY NAVIGATE TO ALL LOCATIONS.

NEIGHBOURHOODS IN DUBLIN

06 MERRION SQUARE & FITZWILLIAM SQUARE

Looking to indulge? The Merrion Square & Fitzwilliam Square area promises a blend of sophistication and charm. Enjoy a stroll through the squares, savour exquisite dishes at top-tier restaurants and stay in luxury accommodation.

07 THE DOCKLANDS

With a mix of old industrial charm and sleek modern architecture, the Docklands offer a more relaxed atmosphere, making it a perfect spot to unwind after a day of sightseeing. Don't worry, you'll still be close enough to the action.

O'Connell Street

One of Dublin's busiest and liveliest streets, it's a hub for some of the city's best food spots. Centrally located, with plenty of nearby museums, theatres and bars there's no shortage of things to explore!

PAGES 42 - 69

O'CONNELL STREET:
Lively streets, foodie spots, theatre shows & museums.

This neighbourhood spans the area north of the Liffey, from Grattan Bridge to Rosie Hackett Bridge, with O'Connell Street at its heart. It's one of Dublin's busiest and most vibrant streets, named after the Irish nationalist legend Daniel O'Connell. Here, Dublin's past and present collide, with towering monuments like the Spire and some of the best food in the city. Whether you're in the mood for museum hopping, diving into hearty Irish grub, or soaking up the craic in local pubs, you'll definitely be spending plenty of time in this lively spot. And if you head a little further north, don't miss the stunning National Botanic Gardens...

TOP 5 THINGS TO SEE & DO

01
GPO MUSEUM

02
14 HENRIETTA STREET

03
HUGH LANE GALLERY

04
CROKE PARK STADIUM & GAA MUSEUM

05
GLASNEVIN: IRELAND'S NATIONAL CEMETERY

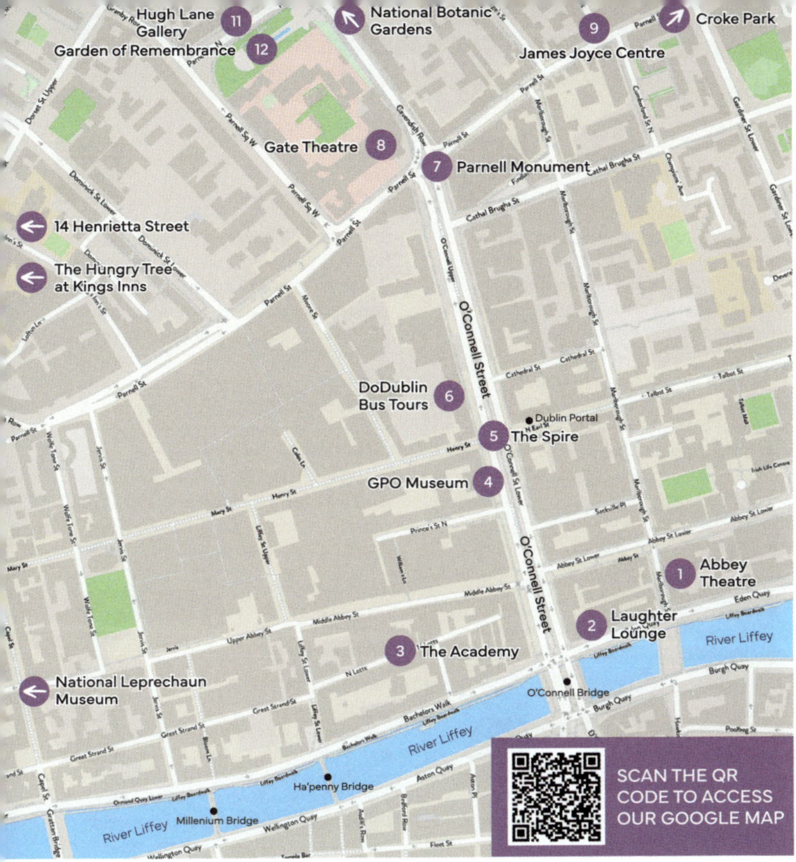

GETTING HERE

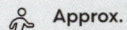 **Approx. Walking Distance From: O'Connell Monument**
Smithfield (22 mins), The Liberties (24 mins), Temple Bar (10 mins), St Stephen's Green (15 mins), Merrion Square (20 mins), Grand Canal Dock (19 mins)

 Luas Tram: Green Line
Stops: O'Connell GPO & O'Connell Upper

 Train Station: Connolly Station
Trains to: Belfast, Sligo, Rosslare, & The Docklands

 Bus Routes to O'Connell Street Lower: 130, 145, 15, 27, 39A, 4, 46A, 784
Stops: Bachelors Walk, Eden Quay, O'Connell Street Lower, Wynn's Hotel

O'CONNELL STREET

THEATRE

Abbey Theatre 1

Best for:
Drama aficionados.
▪ loose.sung.brush

Since its creation in 1904, Dublin's Abbey Theatre (Ireland's National Theatre), has championed Irish artists, showcasing the performances that have shaped the country's artistic identity. For those who want to get a peek behind the curtain, backstage tours are available where you'll learn all about the theatre's storied past and its famed performances. Whether you decide to catch a show or take a tour, it's worth booking in advance. Show tickets are reasonably priced and they offer some concessions.

COMEDY CLUB

Laughter Lounge 2

Best for:
Proper belly laughs.
▪ from.goals.dices

Laying claim to the title of 'Ireland's biggest comedy club', the Laughter Lounge has been cracking up Dubliners for over 25 years. Comedian alumni include Kevin Bridges, Jimmy Carr, and Des Bishop, so you can expect top-notch laughs during your visit! Every Friday and Saturday night, four comedians take to the stage, delivering back-to-back laughs. This one isn't for little ones - there's a strict 18+ policy in place. Be sure to book your tickets in advance through the Laughter Lounge's website.

LIVE MUSIC

The Academy 3

Best for:
Gig goers.
▪ offers.desire.pushy

Since opening in 2007, The Academy has seen some of the best global artists take to its stage. The intimate venue pulls in a wide variety of acts, with previous artists including The Killers, Slayer, Prince and deadmau5 – you can't say that they don't cater to all tastes! With a capacity of just 850, it's the perfect place to experience rising stars up close before they move on to massive stadium shows. And let's face it, everyone wants to claim: "I saw Oasis/Coldplay/Radiohead before they hit the big time!".

MUSEUM · **EDITORS CHOICE**

GPO Museum  4

Best for:
Learning about Irish history.
▪ brands.spend.venue

Visit the award-winning GPO Museum to learn more about Ireland's storied past. The interactive museum focuses on the 1916 Easter Rising, the aftermath of the rebellion and Ireland's fascinating development since. You'll get to learn about the monumental five days of Irish history from eyewitness perspectives, with plenty of engaging and interactive sections to keep all ages interested. The museum is open 7-days a week and we recommend allowing at least an hour for your visit.

MONUMENT

The Spire

  ⑤

Best for:
A quick stop.

drew.colleague.shot

London created the London Eye, Cardiff built the Millennium Stadium and Cornwall developed the Eden Project to celebrate the new Millennia. Dublin's answer? The Spire, a massive 390-foot pin-like monument. While it might not be quite as exciting as the other famous attractions, it's still a pretty impressive sight when wandering down O'Connell Street. As day turns into dusk, the Spire's stainless steel surface is lit both at the base and its tip, so we recommend passing by in the evening, too!

BUS TOUR

DoDublin Bus Tours

⑥

Best for:
A seated tour of Dublin.

dizzy.tour.pace

DoDublin and its expert guides will take you to all the top spots in the city, as you hop-on and hop-off as you please. If you're pushed for time, this can be a great way to cram in as much of Dublin as possible. The buses stop at all the well-known attractions, like the Guinness Storehouse and Dublin Zoo, as well as some hidden gems like Marsh's Library. Kids (under 15) accompanied by adult's travel for free, with the first tour departing at 9am and the final trip finishing at 7pm every day of the week.

The Spire

Hugh Lane Gallery

MONUMENT

Parnell Monument

Best for:
Learning about Irish history.

rips.wrong.adults

Charles Stewart Parnell, once the leader of the Irish Parliamentary Party and a key figure during Ireland's quest for independence, has been immortalised with a 60-foot monument on O'Connell Street. The man that former British Prime Minister, William Gladstone, claimed as 'the most remarkable person he had ever met', still holds a special place in the hearts of many Irish people. Simply head north of the river up O'Connell Street and you'll soon spot the huge bronze statue.

THEATRE

Gate Theatre

Best for:
Stage lovers.

digits.crazy.factor

The Gate Theatre goes beyond just entertaining the people of Dublin, it's a strong part of the local community. Founded in 1928, in the decades since, the theatre has showcased the works of famous Irish authors such as Samuel Beckett and Brian Friel. Performances are broken down into three categories. One covering theatre performances, another the new artistic offerings and the third uses a panel Q&A format to cover pressing issues in the world. Something for everyone!

MUSEUM

James Joyce Cultural Centre

Best for:
Literary lovers.
🔲 shady.leads.aside

Promoting the life, literature and legacy of one of Ireland's, and the world's, greatest writers, the James Joyce Culture Centre is a must-visit for literary and history enthusiasts. Set in an 18th-century townhouse, the centre has plenty of interactive guides, film screenings and courses that will keep any wordsmith entertained for hours. The front door into the museum is actually the very same as Leopold Bloom's, the protagonist of James Joyce's most famous novel, Ulysses – we told you literary lovers will adore this spot!

THEATRE

O'Reilly Theatre

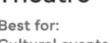 

Best for:
Cultural events.
🔲 fame.cakes.guard

Built within the famous Belvedere College, the O'Reilly Theatre is known for hosting a range of events – from theatre performances to dances to film screenings – there's always something new to see here. Seating around 500 people, with full wheelchair accessibility, productions here feel both intimate and modern. If performances aren't your bag, the theatre also has several sports facilities for hire, including a pool, roofside 5-a-side football pitch, and even a private dining space!

ART GALLERY · **EDITORS CHOICE**

Hugh Lane Gallery

Best for:
Discovering Irish art.
🔲 slips.feared.island

Considered one of Ireland's most important cultural institutions, the gallery is home to a huge range of modern and contemporary Irish and international art. Expect to catch glimpses of work from Ireland's very own Francis Bacon and Sean Scully, as well as a gallery of beautiful stained glass windows. Check out the regularly updated talks the gallery puts on – you might just walk away an inspired artist! Open every day, apart from Mondays, you'll also find a cosy bookshop and café here – perfect for a rainy Dublin day.

GARDEN

Garden of Remembrance

Best for:
Quiet reflection.
🔲 fault.plenty.grid

Opened on the 50th anniversary of the Easter Rising in 1966, the Garden of Remembrance is dedicated to 'all those who gave their lives in the cause of Irish freedom'. Despite being only a stone's throw from the bustle of O'Connell Street, it is a great spot to find some peace and quiet while learning about Irish history. Free to enter, the Garden is open from 8:30am to 6pm during spring and summer before adjusting to the hours of 9.30am to 4pm during autumn and winter.

O'CONNELL STREET

The Gate Theatre

Garden of Remembrance

14 Henrietta Street

| MUSEUM | **EDITORS CHOICE** |

14 Henrietta Street

Best for:
A look into Dublin's past.

camps.rate.wins

When you enter 14 Henrietta Street, you'll get a first-hand look at over 300 years of city life in the walls of just one address. Originally built in the 1720s, by 1911, over 850 people lived on Henrietta Street, with over 100 staying at No. 14. Intimate guided tours help bring to life the everyday realities of Dubliners who called the Georgian building home, painting a picture of how the city has changed over two centuries. Tours run from Wednesday to Sunday and pre-booking via the website is essential.

NATURAL LANDMARK

The Hungry Tree at King's Inns

Best for:
Photo opportunities.

gosh.wage.smashes

Most trees enjoy a steady diet of water, sunshine and carbon dioxide, but one particular tree in Dublin has different tastes, most notably cast iron benches! Found in the grounds of King's Inn, Ireland's oldest law school, instead of growing around a bench, like most trees, the 80-year-old London Plane tree has instead absorbed it into its trunk. Looking like a set piece straight from the Forbidden Forest in Harry Potter, the 'Hungry Tree' is a great spot to snap some pictures!

MUSEUM

National Leprechaun Museum 15

Best for:
Lovers of Irish folklore.
beside.demand.hidden

Yep, you read that right – a Leprechaun museum! The name sounds a bit cheesy doesn't it? Trust us, it's actually a fantastic storytelling tour that's definitely worth a visit. You'll be guided through Irish folklore in quirky rooms filled with creative props. There are two types of tours: the 'Daytime' tour, which is perfect for families and runs every day of the week, and the 'Darkland' tour, which is for 18+ only and runs Thursday to Saturday evenings – so expect a bit of a darker, more mysterious vibe!

RELIGIOUS BUILDING

St Mary's Abbey 16

Best for:
Learning about Dublin Monasteries.
spike.festivity.cook

Founded in 1139, St. Mary's Abbey was one of Ireland's most significant medieval monasteries, although today only the Chapter House and Slype remain. Guided tours offer exclusive access during select times of the year. The Chapter House, where monks once gathered for prayers and councils, is also where Silken Thomas famously renounced his loyalty to Henry VIII in 1534. Access to the Abbey is only available via guided tours which can be booked via Eventbrite during certain times of the year.

ADVENTURE

Axe Club Dublin 17

Best for:
Fun group activity.
slot.verbs.dawn

Perfect for group events or those looking to let off a little steam, Axe Club Dublin will have you feeling like a rugged lumberjack in no time. Expertly guided by axe-throwing instructors (yep, that is a real job), you'll be safely taught how to launch axes at a wooden target, with varying scores depending on your accuracy. All abilities are welcome here, from total beginners to axe-wielding warriors! It's a popular spot so make sure to book in advance to avoid disappointment.

O'CONNELL STREET

The Hungry Tree

National Botanic Gardens

SPORTS ARENA

Croke Park Stadium & GAA Museum

Best for:
Gaelic and hurling aficionados.
■ human.supply.defend

Considered one of Ireland's most iconic sporting venues, Croke Park is one of the biggest sports stadiums in Europe, with a 82,300 capacity! Sadly, 14 civilians were killed here during Bloody Sunday (1920). Today it's home to Gaelic football and hurling, if you're visiting January-August, you might just be able to catch a game at this prestigious venue. Planning your trip after August? Fear not, stadium tours led by passionate guides and access to the GAA Museum can be enjoyed all year round!

ADVENTURE

Skywalk at Croke Park

Best for:
Panoramic views of Dublin.
■ quite.less.tins

Consider yourself a bit of an Evel Knievel? Fan of heights? Looking to impress someone? Well, the Skywalk at Croke Park (or Kellogg's Skyline Croke Park) might just be calling your name! Those brave enough can journey up 17-storeys to the top of Croke Park. From here you'll experience one of, if not the best, vantage points in all of Dublin. The most nerve-wracking moment comes at the 'Pitch View' where you'll have a clear birds eye view of Croke Park below – not for the faint-hearted!

GARDENS

National Botanic Gardens

Best for:
Escaping into nature.
■ rungs.lance.firmly

Found just under 2 miles from the centre of Dublin, the National Botanic Gardens in Glasnevin is the ideal place to escape the hustle and bustle of Ireland's capital. Prepare to take a trip around the globe with over 16,000 plant species from all corners of our planet on display. From the rose garden to the alpine yard to the restored historic greenhouses, plant lovers are sure to love this spot. The gardens are free to enter and remain open every day throughout the year, with varied opening hours based on the seasons.

HISTORICAL CEMETERY

Glasnevin: Ireland's National Cemetery

Best for:
Those interested in Irish icons.
■ harp.liner.plans

OK, so a trip to a cemetery might not seem like an obvious choice but hear us out! Glasnevin is the resting place for more than 1.5 million people, including some Irish greats. It's a must-visit for those interested in the country's history and the guided tours, which can be booked online, are the best way to learn as much as possible. If you have Irish heritage in your family, you can use the on-site computer database to discover more, too! The cemetery and gardens are open 7-days a week, while tours vary depending on the time of year.

O'CONNELL STREET

WALKING TOUR
O'CONNELL STREET

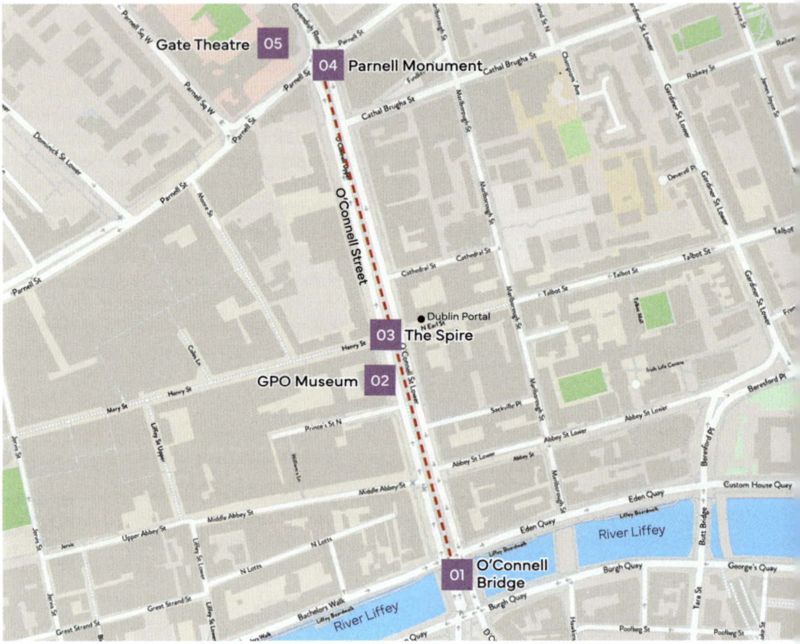

Start your walk at O'Connell Bridge, where Dublin's bustling streets meet the River Liffey. Stroll along the vibrant O'Connell Street, lined with shops, theatres, and historic landmarks. As you walk, admire the towering Spire and the General Post Office. Continue towards the Gate Theatre, one of Dublin's most renowned venues. The walk offers a blend of Dublin's lively atmosphere and cultural heritage.

WALKING TOUR

TOTAL LENGTH: 0.7KM

DURATION: 12 MINS (NO STOPS)

TERRAIN: RELATIVELY FLAT COBBLES

STARTING POINT: O'CONNELL BRIDGE

END POINT: GATE THEATRE

01
O'CONNELL BRIDGE

02
GPO MUSEUM

03
THE SPIRE

04
PARNELL MONUMENT

05
GATE THEATRE

DID YOU KNOW?

Daniel O'Connell, known as the "Liberator," was a leading figure in 19th-century Irish politics. He campaigned tirelessly for Catholic Emancipation, securing the right for Catholics to sit in the British Parliament in 1829. O'Connell was also a strong advocate for Irish independence and human rights, promoting peaceful protest and legal reforms. O'Connell's legacy is celebrated in Dublin, where his statue stands proudly on O'Connell Street - it makes for a great photo!

TIME FOR A BREAK?

Worked up an appetite? Try **BoCo Bar & Oven** for crowd pleasing pizzas and craft drinks. This casual dining spot will certainly not disappoint.

O'CONNELL STREET

MEMORABLE MOMENT:

From folklore to giant chairs, a memorable visit to the National Leprechaun Museum!

BY NO FUSS TRAVEL EDITOR, DANI MAZUR

I have to be honest, I didn't have overly high expectations for this one, Laura and I thought it would be a fun stop to learn more about the tales and mysteries of leprechauns, so we decided to check it out. Now I've got to say, it's a little different to your typical museum experience, with the guide talking you through Irish folklore, whilst journeying through a series of mysterious rooms. After listening to the stories, which were surprisingly interesting *(who knew that fairies were orginally linked with death rather than magic!?)*, the guide unveiled a giant chair. Seems random I know, but it's designed to shrink you down to leprechaun size by sheer scale alone (and it was bigger than it looks in the photo). Being the jokers that we are, Laura and I decided to climb to the top. Just a heads-up, you're allowed to do it, but here's the catch – there's absolutely nothing to help you get up there!

Laura made a few brave attempts but couldn't quite make it. After a bit of teamwork (and a very determined push from Laura), I managed to haul myself up there. Did I look graceful? Absolutely not. I basically starfished

> **❝** It's a little different to your typical museum experience, with the guide talking you through Irish folklore, whilst journeying through a series of mysterious rooms. **❞**

at the top. Once the photo was snapped to prove I made it, there was just one problem left... getting back down. Let's just say my exit strategy was a less graceful descent and more launch yourself into the unknown. Thankfully, no ankles were broken in the process and I could continue exploring the Dublin sites.

So, would I recommend it? Yes, but don't set your expectations too high, it's worth hearing the stories, and going for a laughs, but my advice to you would be bring a climbing buddy for that chair. You'll need them! Also, book the 'Darkland' tour if you want something a little more eerie!

BAR & RESTAURANT

Grand Central

wished.papers.skills

Grand Central dates back to the 19th century when the building was once a grand bank. In 2003, it opened its doors as an eatery but kept its beautiful bank decor – even still with safe doors! Here you can enjoy a range of cuisines from Irish to Asian to finger food.

VEGETARIAN & VEGAN

Govinda's Vegetarian Restaurant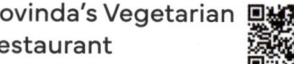

long.humid.mock

Govinda's Restaurant has built itself a beloved following thanks to its affordable prices, big portions and a 100% vegetarian menu (with plant based options). If you've got room after your main course, we highly recommend giving one of their desserts a whirl!

CHOCOLATIER **EDITORS CHOICE**

Butlers Chocolate Café (Henry Street)

cities.pass.tinsel

If you find yourself dreaming of a chocolate induldgence when exploring Dublin, get yourself to Butlers Chocolate Café on Henry Street. This chain of cafés is open 7-days a week offering baked goods, drinks and sugary snacks. You'll even be offered a free chocolate with every hot drink!

DONUTS

The HOT Donut

never.hook.live

Fresh artisan donuts and coffee sound like your kind of thing? Head to The HOT Donut for both sweet and savoury options, from classic strawberry donuts to cheesecake donuts to bacon and cheese donuts! They even offer a wide selection of vegan donuts.

BAR & RESTAURANT

Flanagan's Bar & Restaurant

doctor.exact.oath

A warm and welcoming atmosphere and fresh, locally sourced food – what more could you ask for? This traditional Irish restaurant has been family run since 1980 and offers breakfast, lunch and dinner options. So, if you're after a full Irish or a classic burger, they've got you covered.

Butlers Chocolate Café

PUB (27)

Madigan's Pub O'Connell Street

flips.juices.sits

If you're looking for a good old-fashioned Irish pub, you can't go wrong with a visit to Madigan's Pub O'Connell Street. Serving up hearty traditional Irish food and located near many of the attractions around O'Connell Street, it's an ideal place to refuel and relax!

PUB (28)

Murray's Bar

rabble.blog.asset

Murray's Bar has a rich history dating back to 1797, when its original tavern first opened its doors. Fast forward more than two centuries and it stands strong as a popular sports bar, serving up delicious Irish grub to Dubliners and the capital's visitors within a cosy and comfortable setting.

BAR & GRILL (29)

The Parnell Heritage Bar & Grill

logs.send.motel

The Parnell Heritage Bar & Grill motto is "We celebrate more than just great food and drink; we celebrate Irish history and culture". And boy, do they live up to it! Stop by on a Saturday evening, order a pint of Guinness and Irish stew, and enjoy the sounds of traditional Irish music.

FINE DINING (30)

Restaurant Six

trout.inspector.watch

Looking for somewhere special to eat before attending the theatre? Restaurant Six is situated within Cassidys Hotel, opposite the Gate Theatre, and offers pre-theatre menus. All of their menus are seasonal, using the finest local produce. They're closed Sundays and Mondays.

FINE DINING **LOCALS CHOICE** (31)

Chapter One Restaurant

wide.fence.drape

Laying claim to not one but two Michelin stars, Chapter One delivers an unforgettable fine-dining experience and is a must-visit for serious foodies. Seasonal Irish ingredients take centre stage in its inventive dishes, while the modern art across the interior offers a feast for the eyes, too!

LOCALS CHOICE

"**Chapter One** is a sublime basement Michelin Star restaurant with prices to match. It's worth it, with arty multi-course food concepts drawing on local ingredients, experimental and vibrant. Their spiced twist on Irish coffee particularly shines."

LOCAL WRITER, JAMES HENDICOTT

IRISH/FRENCH FUSION 32
Mr Fox

◼ pocket.treat.assure

Recommended in the Michelin Guide and with over 1,000 five-star customer reviews online, Mr Fox has gained quite a reputation in Dublin. This eatery serves a set menu that changes each month, emphasising seasonality and quality. Walk-ins are welcome but we recommend booking ahead.

COMFORT FOOD 33
Kingfisher Restaurant

◼ thin.transit.beats

A proper Irish 'chippy' serving up big portions of your favourite comfort food. We're talking fish and chips, bangers and mash, apple crumble, knickerbocker glory – everything you need to send yourself into a satisfying food coma after a day of exploring Dublin!

RESTAURANT 34
The Church Café Bar

◼ slope.raves.cute

No prizes to those who guess what this restaurant used to be! The Church is home to over 300 years of Dublin history and is found in a truly stunning Grade I listed building. Not only is the atmosphere and food top-notch, but guests can also enjoy traditional Irish music and dancing every evening!

CHICKEN 35
Mad Egg Millennium Walkway

◼ happen.arts.tidy

The self-proclaimed "#1 Chicken Joint in Ireland". Everything offered at Mad Egg is locally sourced, from the free-range birds hatched locally in a family-run farm, to the bread rolls from Coghlan's bakery to their very own house brew 'Mad Yoke', from Hope Brewery. They offer one veggie option.

CAFÈ 36
Lemon Jelly Cafè

◼ orange.thank.topped

Lemon Jelly Cafè is a spot that takes its food and coffee seriously. From sweet treats to savoury crepes and hearty ciabattas, you won't be leaving here hungry. And if you're looking for a little pick-me-up, Lemon Jelly's ethical coffee will certainly do the trick!

Lemon Jelly Cafè

PantiBar

TEA HOUSE

Tea Garden

cooks.rush.wake

With 6 unique rooms, 40 varieties of global teas and shisha areas to enjoy, it's truly a one-of-a-kind place to visit. Opening in 2008, the founders wanted to create a cool place to hang out with friends, go on dates and experience flavours from around the world. We would say they've absolutely nailed it!

BAKERY & EATERY

The Bakehouse Dublin

paid.nearly.agenda

Fancy a warm cup of coffee, a freshly baked treat or a bowl of homemade soup? Head along the River Liffey, where you'll find The Bakehouse. They offer a wide range of breakfast and lunch options, to enjoy as you look onto the river. They're usually open every day until 3pm.

EATING HOUSE

The Woollen Mills

scale.insect.faced

The perfect people watching spot. Overlook the River Liffey and the iconic Ha'penny Bridge whilst enjoying a cocktail and a bite to eat. The Woollen Mills offers everything from coffee to nachos to fish 'n' chips and fine wines. Head to the roof terrace for a view over Dublin's cityscape.

LGBTQIA+ BAR

PantiBar

headed.formal.empire

Owned by Panti Bliss, LGBTQIA+ activist, performer and the queen of Dublin drag! PantiBar is an LGBTQIA+ venue with a pub vibe and a club atmosphere on the weekends. There are regular DJ sets and you might catch performances from the likes of queens Ariana Grindr and Panti Bliss herself!

BURGERS

Dash Burger

mull.basis.entry

Delicious, well-priced and independently run, Dash Burger is one of Dublin's finest burger joints. The menu keeps it simple with a mouthwatering range of smash burgers, fries to die for and crispy chicken tenders. If you're craving some comfort food, look no further!

JAPANESE & SUSHI

42

Musashi Noodles & Sushi Bar (Capel St)

cubes.dated.mason

Beautifully decorated and serving up tasty Japanese dishes, Musashi is a great choice for those wanting a taste of Asia while in Dublin. Whether you have a hankering for sushi, ramen or stir-fry, all your bases are covered here. A small selection of beer and wine is also on the menu.

Café

43

Brother Hubbard (North)

slick.latter.these

First opening in March 2012, Brother Hubbard now has 4 locations across Dublin. Specialising in fresh, healthy food made from scratch. There's a range of daytime and evening menus available, including a cocktail and beer menu. You'll certainly be spoilt for choice during your visit!

SPEAKEASY BAR — LOCALS CHOICE
44

The Hacienda Bar

along.coach.calls

This hidden gem of a bar is tucked away, to get in you'll have to buzz where you'll receive a warm welcome from the owner (as long as you're up to no trouble). Inside, it's like stepping back in time with pool tables and a juke box. Just remember, it's cash-only, so come prepared!

Brother Hubbard

VEGETARIAN & VEGAN

45

Umi Falafel (Mary Street)

degree.link.apron

100% vegetarian with plenty of vegan options, Umi Falafel has been whipping up fresh, homemade Middle Eastern dishes for Dubliners since 2013. Open 7-days a week from 12pm to 9pm, it's a great spot for lunch or dinner when craving a hearty, healthy dish.

STEAKHOUSE & BAR
46

Bovinity

neon.proven.dizzy

Bovinity is a modern-day steakhouse and cocktail bar that dishes out only the freshest and finest ingredients. From succulent ribeye and pan-fried hake as mains to creamy mash and beef dripping chips as sides, you're bound to leave here with a satisfied stomach!

VIETNAMESE — 47

Aobaba

■ slower.woof.much

For those hankering for genuine Vietnamese food at a great price, Aobaba is here to save the day. Whether it's warming Pho, spicy fried chicken rice or Vietnam's (delicious) take on the sandwich Banh Mi, it serves up authentic flavours that won't break the bank.

KOREAN — 48

Arisu Restaurant

■ foil.shares.comical

Arisu Restaurant brings the traditional taste of Korea to Dublin, complete with authentic Korean furniture and warm service. A meal here starts with complimentary dishes of kimchi, marinated seaweed, and miso soup, followed by the recommended main event, Korean BBQ or fresh sushi.

NEW ORLEANS INSPIRED — 49

Krewe North

■ guides.fully.vanish

With its bright colours, amped-up music, and big flavours, Krewe North offers a feast for most of the senses. The extensive menu has something for everyone, and on Tuesdays, you can dive into the 'Krewe Seafood Boil,' a big ol' shared bowl of lobster, mussels, prawns and more!

VIETNAMESE — 50

Hanoi Hanoi Restaurant

■ humans.sang.expand

Combining great food with a cosy, Vietnamese-inspired atmosphere, a visit here will make you feel like you've flown halfway across the world. Serving up iconic Vietnamese dishes like Phò and Bún Chò as well as Western desserts, it offers something for both savoury and sweet lovers alike.

PIZZA — 51

BoCo Bar + Oven

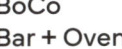

■ loser.tins.prove

Pizza, pizza and more pizza! Oh, and some delicious side options, like their truffled mac n' cheese and woodfired buffalo wings. This casual dining spot cook up your pizza upon order, so your food is super fresh from the woodfired oven. All pizzas can be made with a gluten free base!

O'CONNELL STREET | WHERE TO EAT & DRINK

BoCo

CAFÈ

Lovinspoon

■ acute.scare.frock

Regarded as one of Dublin's cosiest cafès, Lovinspoon is the place to visit if you're on the hunt for a BIG traditional Irish breakfast or a tea and cake stop. The staff are super welcoming and the prices here won't break the bank – what more could you ask for!

PUB

Doyle's Corner

■ pine.panic.logic

Looking like a set straight out of *The Great Gatsby*, Doyle's Corner combines old-school charm with a lively vibe. This popular pub in Phibsborough is a great place to catch up over a drink, watch some live sports and listen to local Dublin musicians every Friday and Saturday night.

MICRO-BAKERY

Sourdough Sisters

■ ripe.rather.lower

Ran by 'two actors who love and eat bread', the Sourdough Sisters pop-up at various markets around the city, where they sell their variety of delicious breads. You can pick up baked goods from their own shop on Drumcondra Road on Thursdays and Fridays ONLY.

MEDITERRANEAN & MIDDLE EASTERN

Shouk

■ beans.cone.puts

All about tasty, healthy food, Shouk sources all of its produce from nearby markets. Blending Mediterranean and Middle Eastern cuisines, the food and atmosphere combine for a great experience. With indoor and outdoor areas, it's ideal for those rare Dublin summer days, as well as the rainy ones.

ITALIAN

Dall'Italiano Restaurant

■ plant.sulk.nerve

With over 1,500 Google Reviews and a 4.9-star rating, Dall'Italiano is a one-man show offering incredible Italian food in a warm, welcoming atmosphere. It's not for rushed dining but perfect for those seeking a unique, personal and unforgettable dining experience!

PUB

John Kavanagh The Gravediggers

■ torn.deck.lions

Founded in 1833 and still family-run, John Kavanagh The Gravediggers has become an iconic Dublin pub. Don't expect razzle-dazzle, big screens or loud music here – this place is all about community and great craic, just what you'd expect from a proper Irish watering hole!

John Kavanagh The Gravediggers

HOTEL 58

The Morrison Dublin

+353 1 887 2400

wire.part.dinner

Add a splash of razzle dazzle to your Dublin trip with a stay at this 5-star hotel. Overlooking the river Liffey, The Morrison Dublin offers all the features of an expensive hotel – we're talking a concierge, fitness centre, room service and plenty more!

HOTEL 59

Hotel Motel One Dublin

+353 1 913 1800

minus.comical.pounds

Motel One Dublin is a modern, affordable hotel just off O'Connell Street, situated near the River Liffey. It features stylish design, a bar and pet-friendly rooms. Dogs must be booked in ahead, there's an additional charge of €15 per dog per day.

APARTHOTEL 60

Zanzibar Locke

+353 1 436 3700

hush.helps.slim

Bridging the gap between travel and home comforts, they offer luxury hotel accommodation within private apartments. Travelling with your four-legged pal? One dog under 20kg is allowed per room, and bowls and beds are available on request.

HOTEL 61

Wynn's Hotel

+353 1 874 5131

alien.sushi.status

If you're visiting Dublin to learn about its history, a stay at Wynn's Hotel should definitely be on the cards. Established in 1845 and housed within a listed building, this hotel is brimming with Dublin lore. Book direct and you'll get breakfast included.

APARTHOTEL 62

Staycity Aparthotels Dublin

+353 1 556 7531

power.loose.market

If a home away from home is your style, this is the place for you. Each studio and apartment is fitted with a kitchen, dining area and comfy beds, while the building includes a gym and a laundry room – everything you could need!

HOTEL 63

Point A Dublin Parnell Street

+353 1 221 0400

swim.salon.depend

If you're looking for a modern yet affordable hotel to lay your head on Parnell Street, you can't go wrong with Point A. Make sure to book directly, that way you'll get to pick your room and get 10% off, as well as a free breakfast!

HOTEL

Hotel Riu Plaza The Gresham Dublin

+353 1 874 6881

inform.hunt.social

This hotel combines modern convenience with old-fashioned charm. Set in a beautifully restored 19th-century building, this 4-star hotel has recently undergone an extensive refurbishment, so expect top quality comfort during your stay!

HOTEL

Holiday Inn Express Dublin City Centre
+353 1 878 8099

double.family.maker

A basic but modern hotel with all the amenities needed for a short trip on a budget, you can't go wrong with a stay at this Holiday Inn Express. Take full advantage of the free breakfast to fuel a day of exploration, too! Just note that the rooms do lack storage space.

HOTEL

Maldron Hotel Parnell Square
+353 1 871 6800

spill.hidden.text

Just a 3-minute walk to O'Connell Street, this 4-star hotel is a great base to explore the city. The friendly team here also offers reduced rate packages, including two and three-night stay deals to help you keep your budget down!

Zanzibar Locke

HOTEL

Hotel 7 Dublin
+353 1 873 7777

lost.enhancement.fever

Hotel 7 Dublin is a cosy place to stay that mixes modern features with a classic, elegant aesthetic. Rooms range from singles up to triples and include rainfall showers, air-con and even a Nespresso machine! There's also an on-site restaurant and bar.

Smithfield & Stoneybatter

Smithfield and Stoneybatter are among Dublin's trendiest and most contemporary hangouts, known for their independent cafés, Irish pubs, and top-tier restaurants. You'll also find some key attractions in the area.

PAGES 70 - 91

SMITHFIELD & STONEYBATTER:
Dublin's trendiest hangout spots.

Smithfield and Stoneybatter have really reinvented themselves, shifting from their historic market roots to become two of Dublin's coolest, most vibrant spots. Now, you'll find everything from the almost 250-year-old Jameson Distillery, where you can enjoy top-notch tours and tastings, to the family-friendly Dublin Zoo, home to all sorts of animals. Smithfield Square is the perfect place for a wander, with cobbled streets full of cosy cafés, proper Irish pubs, and amazing restaurants. You can also climb the Skyview Tower for jaw-dropping views or head to Phoenix Park for a peaceful escape. Whether you're after great pubs, fun activities, or some time in nature, Smithfield and Stoneybatter have got you covered! Just a little west, you'll also find Phoenix Park…

TOP 5 THINGS TO SEE & DO

01
JAMESON DISTILLERY BOW ST.

02
PHOENIX PARK

03
DUBLIN ZOO

04
NATIONAL MUSEUM OF IRELAND

05
SKYVIEW TOWER

SCAN THE QR CODE TO ACCESS OUR GOOGLE MAP

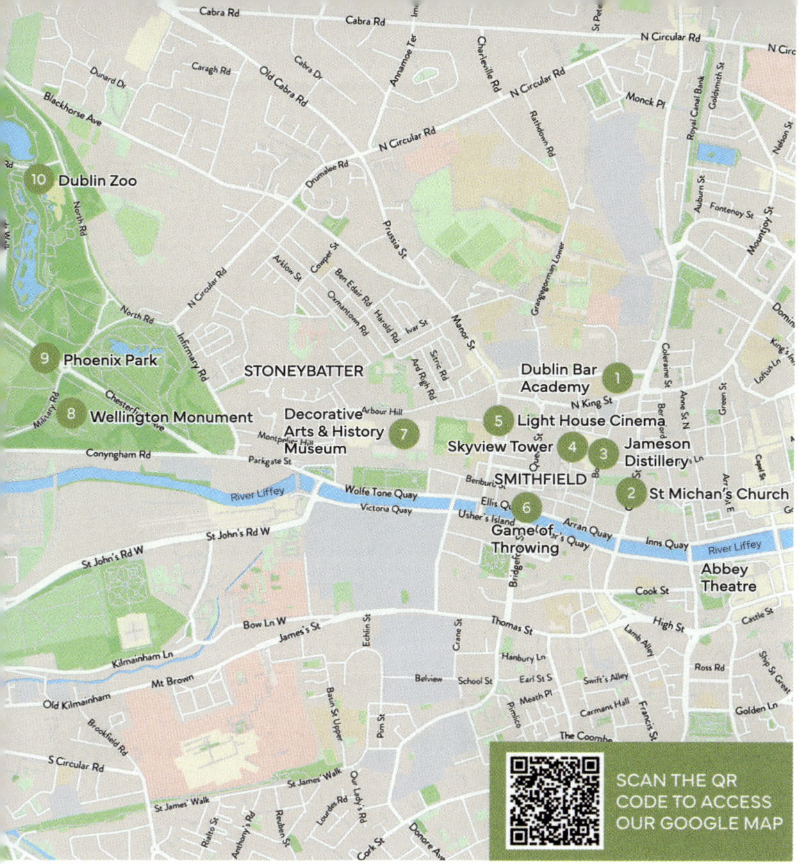

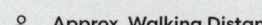

GETTING HERE

Approx. Walking Distance From: Smithfield
O'Connell St (22 mins), The Liberties (12 mins), Temple Bar (16 mins), St Stephen's Green (33 mins), Merrion Square (38 mins), Grand Canal Dock (41 mins)

Luas Tram: Red Line
Stops: Smithfield & Museum

Bus Routes to Smithfield: 145, 26, 39, 39A, 69, 70, C1, S2
Stops: Smithfield, Arran Quay, St Michan's Church, Blackhall Place (Stoneybatter)

Jameson Distillery Bow St.

WORKSHOP

Dublin Bar Academy

Best for:
Cocktail connoisseurs.
defeat.tiles.heats

Have you got a couple of free days and a passion for cocktails? The Dublin Bar Academy's 2-day 'Cocktails & Mixology Course' might just be the perfect way to shake things up! Run by experienced instructors in a real bartender school, the course covers all the mixology essentials and will have you confidently shaking, stirring and pouring like a pro. Perfect for beginners or enthusiasts, you'll leave the course with mixology skills guaranteed to wow friends and family at your next party.

RELIGIOUS LOCATION

St Michan's Church

Best for:
A creepy history lesson.
seats.crazy.debate

Dating back to 1095, St Michan's Church has been witness to much of Ireland's fascinating past. Despite its modest appearance, if you travel down some steep, narrow steps you'll discover one of Dublin's creepiest attractions. Underground crypts with open caskets house several influential families. These vaults and mummified bodies are even said to have inspired Bram Stoker's Dracula! Note, that the church is closed Friday to Sunday, public holidays, and bank holidays.

DISTILLERY

EDITORS CHOICE

Jameson Distillery Bow St.

Best for:
Those who enjoy a tipple or two.

▪ dent.online.rider

Founded by John Jameson in 1780, this former factory (that stopped production in 1971), today remains open offering visitors 'world-leading' distillery tours from informative and friendly-faced guides. The Jameson Distillery Bow St. offer a variety of tours and experiences to choose from (all at varying prices) including cocktail making classes, premium whiskey tasting sessions and lessons in blending your own whiskey. We would recommend booking tours in advance.

VIEWPOINT

Skyview Tower

Best for:
360° views of Dublin.

▪ dined.mouth.forget

Once a chimney for Jameson Whiskey and one of Dublin's tallest structures, the Skyview Tower now offers spectacular city views. With 259 steps and a height of 220 feet, it's not for the faint-hearted (we speak from experience). But for those who are daring enough to make the journey, your reward is a panoramic view of the city. To secure entry to the tower, you'll need to head to the Generator Hostel next door to purchase a ticket – just some friendly advice, as we had some trouble finding it ourselves!

CINEMA

Light House Cinema

Best for:
Rainy days.

▪ hosts.palace.speeds

Light House Cinema is a proud independent movie theatre located a short walk from the River Liffey. Across its four screens and 614 seats guests can experience a real eclectic range of films – from Irish releases to Hollywood blockbusters to feature-length documentaries. Perfect for grabbing a bite before the film or engaging in that essential post-film analysis, the on-site bar and café is the ideal spot for moviegoers to unwind and chat! Accessible and sensory screenings are hosted here. Find more information online.

ADVENTURE

Game of Throwing

Best for:
Letting off some steam.

▪ pile.served.limbs

Re-invigorating the world of axe throwing, Game of Throwing goes beyond simply lobbing an axe into a wooden board. Here visitors have the choice of multiple interactive lanes, all with their own games and challenges. It's a great group activity, and we had a lot of fun giving it a go ourselves. Although, we did get a little competitive and let's just say some of the team members were more successful than others at hitting the target! It's open 7-days a week and tickets are best bought online, guests also need to be 10 years or older to participate.

SMITHFIELD & STONEYBATTER

Skyview Tower

Jameson Distillery Bow St.

MUSEUM

National Museum of Ireland - Decorative Arts & History

 7

Best for:
Art & history lovers.

belong.honey.transfers

For a fascinating journey through Ireland's past, head to the National Museum of Ireland - Decorative Arts & History. Housed in a historic military building, the museum showcases everything from Irish silver, furniture and costume to captivating artefacts covering Irish military history. Highlights include the "Proclaiming a Republic" exhibition, which explores the 1916 Easter Rising. Entry is free and the museum is open 7-days a week, it's an easy, budget-friendly activity for all ages.

National Museum of Ireland

MONUMENT

Wellington Monument

 8

Best for:
Picnics & walks.

known.clever.labs

Standing at a mighty 203 feet, the monument is the largest obelisk in Europe and has held pride of place in Phoenix Park since 1861. The monument was built in honour of Irish-born Arthur Wellesley, the Duke of Wellington, who defeated Napoleon at the Battle of Waterloo, served as a member of Parliament and eventually went on to be Prime Minister of England. Being set inside the beautiful Phoenix Park, the monument is a great spot for a picnic during the warmer months or a gentle stroll as the seasons change.

PUBLIC PARK

Phoenix Park

  9

Best for:
A place to walk & unwind.

after.mirror.blunt

Phoenix Park spreads across 1,750 acres *(twice the size of New York's Central Park)* and is the perfect spot to get away from the lively city centre. There are lots of routes to walk or cycle *(bike rental is available)*, look out for the herd of deer that roam freely within the park. The park has a lot to offer including multiple monuments, cafés and a visitor centre. It's also home to the Farmleigh Estate, Dublin Zoo and Áras an Uachtaráin (the official residence of the Irish president).

ZOO

Dublin Zoo

Best for:
Animal lovers.
◼ term.dots.sailor

Spanning over 70 acres and home to more than 400 animals, Dublin Zoo is a must-visit for wildlife enthusiasts. First opened in 1831, it ranks among the world's oldest and most popular zoos, home to creatures big and small – from playful orangutans to charming red pandas and graceful sea lions. Easily accessible by car and bus, the zoo offers plenty of engaging *'keeper talks'* along with rotating workshops and lectures. Discounted rates are available for bookings made at least five days ahead.

WATERSPORTS

Rafting.ie

Best for:
Adventure seekers.
◼ losses.staple.wiring

Just 15 minutes from the city centre, Rafting.ie and its expert team offer an unforgettable two-and-a-half-hour tour through Dublin's waterways. Navigate rapids and weirs over 5-miles through the scenic Strawberry Beds, as your on-board guide points out fascinating wildlife and historic landmarks along the way. Tours run 7-days a week and are suitable for those 11 years old and above, with tickets starting from €55 per person when booked online. Wetsuits and helmets are provided.

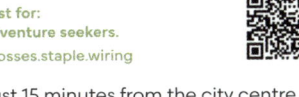

Phoenix Park

WALKING TOUR
SMITHFIELD & STONEYBATTER

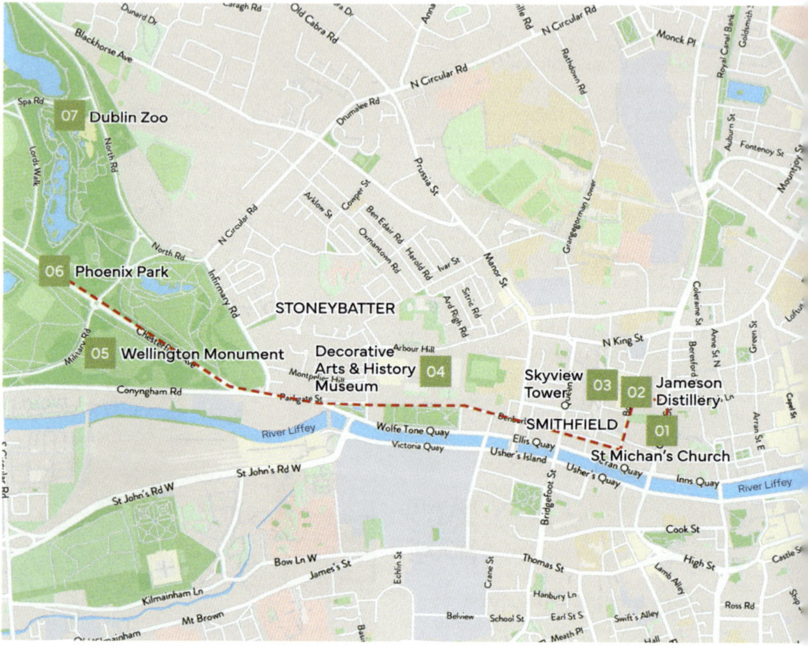

Start in Smithfield, Dublin's historic market district, where you can admire the old-fashioned architecture and vibrant atmosphere. Pass by the iconic Jameson Distillery, where you can learn about the art of whiskey making. Continue through Stoneybatter, a charming neighbourhood filled with pubs and local shops. The route culminates at Dublin Zoo, where you can explore lush landscapes and diverse wildlife.

WALKING TOUR

TOTAL LENGTH: 3.2KM
DURATION: 45 MINS (NO STOPS)
TERRAIN: RELATIVELY FLAT
STARTING POINT: ST MICHAN'S CHURCH
END POINT: DUBLIN ZOO

01
ST MICHAN'S CHURCH

06
PHOENIX PARK

02
JAMESON DISTILLERY

07
DUBLIN ZOO

03
SKYVIEW TOWER

04
DECORATIVE ARTS & HISTORY MUSEUM

05
WELLINGTON MONUMENT

TIME FOR A BREAK?

Worked up an appetite? Recharge at **Nutbutter** with some wholesome goodness—the perfect spot for a casual lunch. Also a firm favourite among the No Fuss team.

SMITHFIELD & STONEYBATTER

MEMORABLE MOMENT:

A rainy day in Smithfield & Stoneybatter, followed by an action-packed evening of axe throwing!

BY NO FUSS TRAVEL EDITOR, DANI MAZUR

Let's set the scene, we wake up in Dublin to the freezing cold January weather, grey skies and a forecast of rain, which is expected to last all day! Despite the grim weather, we decided to head to Urbanity in Smithfield for a much-needed breakfast to fuel us for the day ahead. It was delicious, and let's just say we were going to need it more than we realised...

So, one of us, well either Laura or Ryan - I can't remember who, but it certainly couldn't have been me - thought it would be a great idea to head to the nearby Skyview Tower *(which was once a chimney for the Jameson Distillery)* and climb the tower's spiral staircase, which included 259 steps! I'm all for a panoramic view of the city, but it didn't quite have the same appeal in the rain.

After clambering to the top *(all 220 feet of it!)*, out of breath and with Laura feeling dizzy, we made it. Despite the weather, the views were incredible and stretched for miles –

imagine how much better they'd be on a clear day! After grabbing some photos, we headed back down to explore more of the area. Soaked from the rain, we found a spot (Green Door Bakery) to grab a much-needed cuppa and a sweet treat. Then, we explored the National Museum of Ireland – Decorative Arts and History, perfect for a rainy-day activity.

Later, we met up with the group for an evening meal at Nutbutter, which I'd highly recommend if you're in the mood for some wholesome goodness. The night ended with a competitive game of axe throwing. Turns out, it wasn't as competitive as I'd hoped, as, simply put, I was rubbish – but I gave it my best shot. It came down to Rob and Ryan battling it out, with Ryan eventually being crowned the winner.

To celebrate, where else could we go but the aptly named Frank Ryan's Bar for a well-earned Guinness? If you visit, it's a quirky spot – very dark, with pictures and ornaments scattered all over the place. They also serve stone-baked pizza slices, and just to add, there's a dog roaming around – we wouldn't want you tripping over him in the dark!

COFFEE SHOP   12

Copper + Straw Speciality Coffee

◼ atoms.count.guards

After spending countless hours in coffee shops trying to make it as a writer, Stephen Kennedy realised his passion wasn't for the written word but for the coffee bean. Copper & Straw was born, where you can get unbelievable brews and plenty of tasty treats, including gluten-free and vegan options.

CAFÉ 13

Cinnamon Café

◼ nurse.extra.riots

A café oozing with the charm and atmosphere that corporate chains can only dream of, Cinnamon Café is a great spot to grab a quick bite to eat on a Dublin day out. Whether you're up for a fried breakfast, a baked treat or just a good old cup of coffee, you're sorted here.

CAFÉ 14

Urbanity

◼ trend.former.orange

Known for its specialty coffee and seasonal locally sourced menus, Urbanity is one of Smithfield's coolest cafés. Open 7-days a week, its bright, modern interior and relaxed vibe make it a top tier choice for brunch or a quick stop-off between attractions.

JAPANESE 15

Matsukawa

◼ skinny.happen.drop

With only eight seats available, a meal at Matsukawa is an intimate experience. The team here serve omakase (which translates to 'leave it to the chef'), with 18 incredible dishes prepared right in front of you. Pre-book well ahead – this spot is small, exclusive and seriously in demand!

PUB & PIZZA 16

Frank Ryan's Bar

◼ swan.fool.weep

A character-filled spot perfect for grabbing a pizza and a pint. Known for its dark, atmospheric charm and alleged hauntings, the bar's walls are adorned with an eclectic mix of pictures and ornaments. Don't let the dim lighting spook you— it's great for those seeking a quirky pub visit.

BAR, RESTAURANT & VENUE   17

Fidelity

◼ toast.tribal.added

If you're someone who loves high-quality music, beers and bar snacks, boy oh boy, do we have the spot for you. Fidelity boasts one of Ireland's best sound systems, paired with an extensive drinks menu and Asian-inspired bites that take bar food to a whole new level.

RESTAURANT 18

PHX Bistro

cheer.thigh.fairly

PHX Bistro is a small family-run eatery with heaps of charm and a menu to match. Here you can grab two or three course meals every night of the week for under €40, with a decent choice ranging from fish to steak to risotto. They also offer a lunch menu from 12pm-4pm, 7-days a week.

FISH & CHIPS 19

Fish Shop

café.erase.acid

Fish Shop might be small in size, but it's a giant among seafood aficionados. Striking the perfect balance between upmarket dining and a classic fish and chip shop, it offers snacks, mains (gluten free options) and puddings, along with a substantial wine list to wash it all down!

COFFEE SPECIALISTS 20

Proper Order Coffee Co & No Messin' Bakery

into.belts.gears

Think science lab meets café when it comes to this place. If delicate, subtle flavours are more your thing than the sweet, syrupy stuff found in big-name chains, Proper Order won't disappoint. You can also pick up some seriously tasty baked treats from the in-house No Messin Bakery!

RESTAURANT & COMMUNITY SPACE 21

Third Space

places.speaks.reach

Serving big ol' fried breakfasts, homemade pastries and toasted sandwiches, Third Space is more than just an eatery. It's all about providing community space for locals and visitors to get together and enjoy good food in good company. With loneliness on the rise, this is a worthy cause to get behind!

FLEXITARIAN   22

Nutbutter Smithfield

goat.hooks.spell

Proudly living the 'flexitarian dream,' the owner set out to create a restaurant where visitors could enjoy both a tasty plant-based dish and slow-cooked brisket on the same menu. All food served here is made from scratch and sourced from fresh, ethically sourced Irish ingredients.

Nutbutter

IRISH/ITALIAN RESTAURANT — 23

Sparks Bistro

firm.expand.monday

Sparks Bistro mixes Irish charm with Italian flair, serving hearty, flavour-packed dishes that celebrate both traditions. With a relaxed atmosphere, welcoming staff and central location, it's an ideal spot for a casual meal or a romantic night out!

BRUNCH — 24

Mad Yolks

modes.tower.animal

Located near the Jameson Distillery, this spot is great for a quick brunch bite. You might have guessed, as the name suggests, everything pretty much contains eggs! Sandwiches from the Yolko Ono, to the Mad Yolk and the Buff Yolk, plus tasty sides like hash browns and halloumi fries.

BAR & RESTAURANT — 25

Oscars Café Bar

liner.healthier.puns

Serving modern and classic European dishes 7-days a week, a visit here should always be on the to-do list when in Dublin. This is a great spot to enjoy al fresco dining during the summer months, with a fantastic outdoor eating area right in the centre of Smithfield Square.

BBQ — 26

My Meat Wagon

chart.duty.sums

My Meat Wagon is a no-nonsense Texas BBQ spot that delivers on portions, taste and atmosphere. This laid-back smoke joint offers a simple menu done incredibly well. Pick from 'cow, pig or bird', some sauces and a bunch of traditional sides, and the next thing you know, you're in BBQ heaven!

PUB — LOCALS CHOICE — 27

The Cobblestone

poetic.chop.quite

For over 35 years, the Cobblestone has championed traditional Irish music and cemented itself as one of Dublin's most iconic pubs. Stop by any day of the week for live tunes from some of Ireland's finest musicians. Check out their 'session etiquette' online ahead of visiting.

LOCALS CHOICE

"**The Cobblestone Pub** recently succeeded in a vocal campaign to avoid being turned into a hotel. The passion is easily understood: this roughshod, 70s-feel, lounge pub is Dublin's best (mostly) tourist-free trad music spot. Think fading cushioned seats and bearded foot-tapping musicians, and remember, for the bathrooms, Mná means woman, not man!"

LOCAL WRITER, JAMES HENDICOTT

CAFÉ & GROCER

Lilliput Stores

divide.rips.policy

Lilliput Stores is a proudly Irish-owned and operated artisan café, eatery and grocer, that specialise in both Irish and Mediterranean artisan foods - quite the combo! Opening its doors in 2007, it's built a reputation for serving bold and flavourful coffee, as well as toasties and brunch options.

CAFÉ

Social Fabric Café

bench.forms.woods

Having transformed from a post office to a welcoming eatery, Social Fabric Café traded those never-ending post office queues for a warm, cosy atmosphere. Pet-friendly and community-focused, it's perfect for everything from relaxed brunches to grabbing some coffee on the go.

CHINESE

Hakkahan

alone.nerve.fuel

Hakkahan bucks the trend of most Chinese restaurants and offers a smaller menu that has been honed to perfection. If you're into spice, the 'Sichuan' section is where you'll want to order. Prefer to keep things mild? No problem, there are plenty of options that won't have your ears steaming.

PUB

The Glimmer Man

smug.ships.quite

A Stoneybatter stalwart since 1989, The Glimmer Man offers comfy corners designed for unwinding after a day on your feet. Thanks to its quirky interior, dog-friendly policy and the Vietnam food truck in the back, it's always lively here. Just a heads up – cash only here, but an on-site ATM is available!

VIETNAMESE

Vietnam Dublin

cups.copies.bend

Hidden in the pub garden of The Glimmer Man you'll find Vietnam Dublin, a beloved independent Vietnamese-inspired food truck. Open Thursday evening to Sunday, this eatery specialises in mouthwatering Banh Mi's (Vietnam's take on a sandwich) and fragrant jasmine rice bowls.

CHICKEN RESTAURANT

All Bar Chicken

issues.caring.oddly

Billed as the 'ultimate dine and disco destination', All Bar Chicken combines nostalgia with poultry perfection. A visit here involves tucking into delicious dishes surrounded by iconic film posters, while classic hits from the 80s to noughties blast through the speakers – what more could you want?

PUB LOCALS CHOICE 34

L.Mulligan Grocer

swift.agenda.oven

L. Mulligan Grocer dishes up hearty, Irish-inspired meals paired with an impressive selection of craft beers and whiskeys. Known for its cosy, unpretentious vibe, this gastropub combines locally sourced ingredients with a welcoming atmosphere, offering a true taste of proper Irish food.

ITALIAN LOCALS CHOICE 35

Grano

frogs.engine.chief

Grano Italian sources only fresh, organic ingredients and wines from authentic regional suppliers. Expect top-notch presentation, extremely high attention to detail and flavours out of this world. Just a heads up, this place is popular, and you'll need to book a good few weeks (at least!) in advance.

WINE BAR 36

A Fianco

runner.suffer.supper

If you're into great wine and Italian food (and let's be honest, who isn't?), A Fianco is a must. With organic wines farmed using 'old techniques' and small but flavour-packed Italian dishes, A Fianco promises a feast your taste buds won't forget! They're closed on Mondays.

BAKERY 37

Green Door Bakery

civil.rivers.perky

Found a little off-the-beaten-path for tourists, Green Door Bakery is a great spot to escape the crowds and indulge in a sweet bite (or three!). The bread here is incredibly soft and fluffy while the coffee, cinnamon rolls and other baked delights go down a treat, too!

RESTAURANT 38

SLICE

secure.belong.homes

SLICE champions small suppliers, serving up seasonal dishes that are perfect for breakfast, lunch or something in between! From fresh salads to buttermilk pancakes to the soup of the day (complete with Guinness bread!), every dish feels like a slice of comfort here.

COFFEE SHOP 39

Joli

agreed.global.flags

Joli's mission is simple: serve great coffee, treats and hot food to the local community and beyond. Open every day of the week, grab breakfast or lunch, a cuppa and a few tasty sweet and savoury snacks for the road (fresh sandwiches and sausage rolls are made in house every day!).

KOREAN — 40

Korean Table

 soup.level.star

Starting out as a food stall at a Dublin market, Korean Table has grown into one of the city's premier spots for bold, authentic Asian flavours. The restaurant only accepts walk-ins (unless you're a group of 10 or more) and is open Tuesday to Sunday. The slow cooked beef ribs are a firm favourite.

CAFÉ — 41

The Little Cactus

 gallons.tamed.puzzle

The Little Cactus is the epitome of a cosy café, inspired by its owners' time in Vancouver, Canada, and the city's trendy coffee spots. They realised Dublin was missing a place where you could grab great coffee, pick up some vintage clothing and, of course, admire some cacti!

PUB — 42

Hynes Bar

 grass.burst.wacky

Hynes Bar boasts a beautifully restored interior, a beer garden and a great line-up of local beers. A warm welcome extends to our four-legged friends too! While the pub doesn't serve food, visitors are encouraged to grab some Vietnamese dishes from next door (The Streets) and enjoy them here.

INDIAN — 43

Indian Zaika

 former.dawn.hips

Indian Zaika serves up authentic Indian cuisine with rich, bold flavours crafted by five-star chefs. Open daily for dinner and weekends for lunch, this local favourite offers both dine-in and takeaway options. Their meats are sourced from Halal Certified Suppliers.

VICTORIAN PUB — LOCALS CHOICE — 44

Ryan's Parkgate Street

 shapes.jacket.slices

A beautifully restored Victorian public house, complete with original features like gas lamps, whiskey barrels, tea drawers and traditional snugs. Whether you're looking for a hearty meal in the restaurant and grill room or a perfect pint of Guinness at the Victorian bar, Ryan's offers the best of both worlds.

CAFÉ — 45

DASH Container Café

 design.deeper.judge

Born out of the pandemic, Dash-Container quickly became the go-to coffee spot when indoor dining was off the table. Since then it's grown from strength to strength, and that will come as no surprise when you look at its amazing menu, great coffee and dog-friendly policy!

HOTEL 46

Maldron Hotel Smithfield

+353 1 485 0900

 lifted.policy.words

This hotel offers a contemporary stay with 92 rooms, many featuring floor-to-ceiling windows or balconies offering panoramic city views. With the welcoming on-site Grain & Grill restaurant and easy access to public transport, it's an ideal choice for a hassle-free stay.

BOUTIQUE HOTEL 47

McGettigan's Townhouse

+353 1 699 3310

 cabin.sleep.stand

With a lively pub downstairs, a central location in Smithfield and comfy, cosy rooms, McGettigan's Townhouse has everything you could want from a small Dublin hotel that blends traditional Irish charm with modern amenities.

HOTEL 48

The Hendrick Smithfield

+3531 482 6500

 awards.cook.congratulations

The Hendrick Smithfield offers a modern, minimalist stay just steps from Dublin's lively markets, pubs and attractions. Its art-filled interior and bar reflect Smithfield's growing reputation as Dublin's coolest district. Pizzas and snacks are available at the bar.

HOTEL   49

easyHotel Dublin City Centre

+353 1 539 2909

 rounds.charge.expose

easyHotel Dublin City Centre offers budget-friendly accommodation in a central location, perfect for exploring Dublin's sights. The modern, minimalist rooms include essential amenities, with everything you need to recharge and unwind after a day in the city.

HOTEL 50

Ashling Hotel Dublin

+353 1 677 2324

 grit.senior.kicked

An award-winning 4-star hotel adjacent to Heuston Station, not only is this hotel situated in a great spot, but they go above and beyond for their guests. It is the first hotel in Dublin to open sensory guest rooms, ensuring a soothing stay for all.

McGettigan's Townhouse

The Liberties & Kilmainham

Love a good tipple? Then this is the spot for you! The birthplace of Guinness and home to whiskey distilleries like Roe & Co, Teeling and Pearse Lyons, it has plenty to offer. It also has historic landmarks such as Kilmainham Gaol and Marsh's Library.

THE LIBERTIES & KILMAINHAM:
The birthplace of Guinness.

The Liberties & Kilmainham area is where Dublin's historic charm meets its lively, spirited side. Known as the birthplace of Guinness and home to iconic whiskey distilleries like Roe & Co, Teeling, and Pearse Lyons, it's a must-visit if you love a good tipple. But it's not just about the booze – you'll also find a mix of fascinating attractions, from the Irish Museum of Modern Art to Kilmainham Gaol, plus brilliant spots to eat, drink, and unwind. Whether you're a whiskey lover (Sláinte!), a history buff, or just keen to explore Dublin's vibrant streets, this area has something for everyone!

TOP 5 THINGS TO SEE & DO

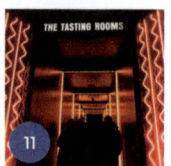

01
GUINNESS STOREHOUSE

02
TEELING WHISKEY DISTILLERY

03
KILMAINHAM GAOL

04
DUBLINIA VIKING MUSEUM

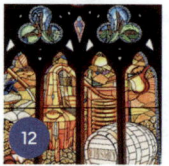

05
PEARSE LYONS WHISKEY DISTILLERY

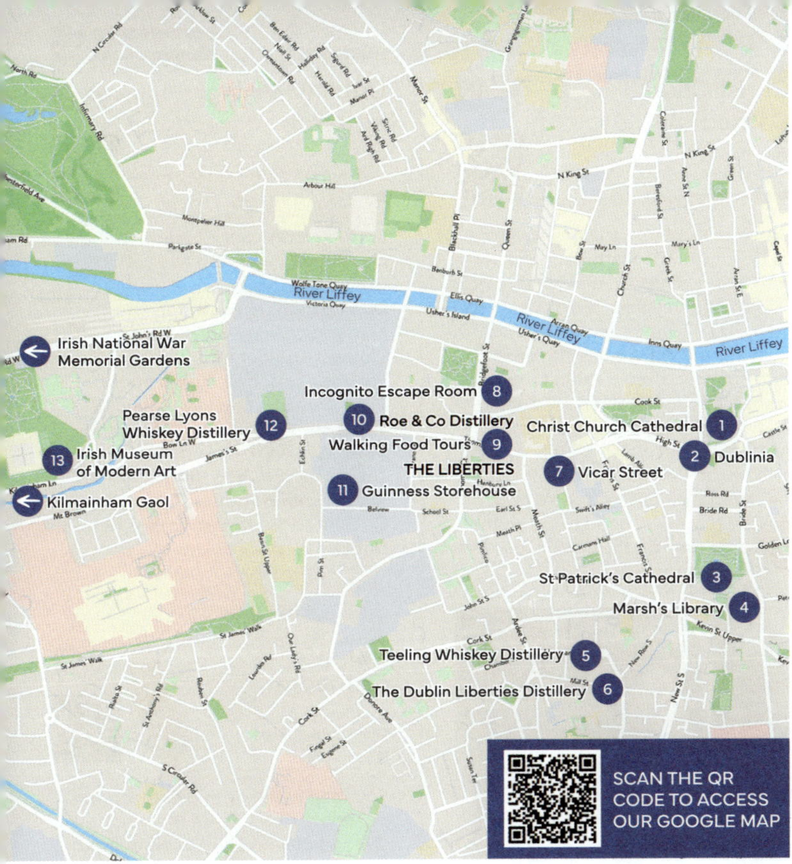

GETTING HERE

🚶 **Approx. Walking Distance From: The Liberties**
O'Connell St (24 mins), Smithfield (12 mins), Temple Bar (15 mins), St Stephen's Green (25 mins), Merrion Square (37 mins), Grand Canal Dock (40 mins)

🚋 **Luas Tram: Red Line**
Stops: James's (Liberties) & Suir Road (Kilmainham)

🚌 **Bus Routes to The Liberties: 13, 145, 150, 27, 39, 783**
Stops: Thomas Street, St Luke's Avenue, Ardee Court, Dean Street, St Patrick's Cathedral

THE LIBERTIES & KILMAINHAM

RELIGIOUS LOCATION

Christ Church Cathedral

  1

Best for:
History lovers.

forces.length.bits

Dive into Dublin's rich history with a visit to Christ Church Cathedral or appreciate the buildings stunning architecture from afar (if religious buildings aren't your thing). The cathedral was first constructed in the early 11th century and houses different exhibits, the world's highest number of swinging bells and, if you're brave enough to enter the crypt, you'll even find a mummified cat! Self-guided tickets can be purchased online, if you'd prefer a guided tour you'll need to ask at the welcome desk on the day of your visit.

Teeling Whiskey Distillery

MUSEUM   **EDITORS CHOICE**

Dublinia Viking Museum

  2

Best for:
Unique, family-friendly experience.

leaves.quench.raves

Looking for a family-friendly or rainy-day activity? Or want to see Dublin from a new perspective? Head to Dublinia, where you'll step into Medieval Viking Dublin - try on Viking clothes, experience a bustling medieval street, discover life on-board a Viking warship and learn about the impacts the Vikings had in Ireland. Make sure you head up St Michael's Tower whilst visiting (although you'll need to climb 96 stairs!), where you'll be treated to sweeping views across Dublin. Pre-book tickets online.

RELIGIOUS LOCATION

St Patrick's Cathedral

  3

Best for:
Quiet contemplation.

gained.pint.lungs

Founded in 1191, with a history dating as far back as 450 AD, St Patrick's Cathedral is one of the few buildings left from the medieval city of Dublin. This awe-inspiring Gothic structure is Ireland's largest cathedral, attracting visitors worldwide with its soaring arches, intricate stained glass and long history. Highlights include the tomb of Jonathan Swift, author of Gulliver's Travels and a former dean, along with daily guided tours (except Sundays). Concessions for students, families and seniors are available.

Dublinia Viking Museum

LIBRARY

Marsh's Library ④

Best for:
Stepping back in time.
▫ text.drain.safely

Dating back to 1707, Marsh's Library is the oldest public library in Ireland and is one of the few buildings still used for its original purpose (with desks and books in the same place they were 200 years ago). Books were donated to the library in the early 18th century and are very rare and valuable, today the library holds 25,000 books, as well as 300 manuscripts. There's a small entry fee, however, seniors and under 18's go free. You can book in advance online or pay on entry.

DISTILLERY

Teeling Whiskey Distillery ⑤

Best for:
Tours & tasting.
▫ broom.type.voter

The Teeling Whiskey Distillery only began production in 2015. It will be several years before any of the distillate can be called whiskey but, in the meantime, visitors can enjoy tours of the fully operational distillery in action (not every 'distillery 'in the city is a working one), and taste and buy whiskeys from the family's other distillery which is located on the Cooley Peninsula. Prices vary depending on your chosen tour, we would recommend booking in advance, as we did. Dogs are ONLY welcome in the on-site Phoenix Café.

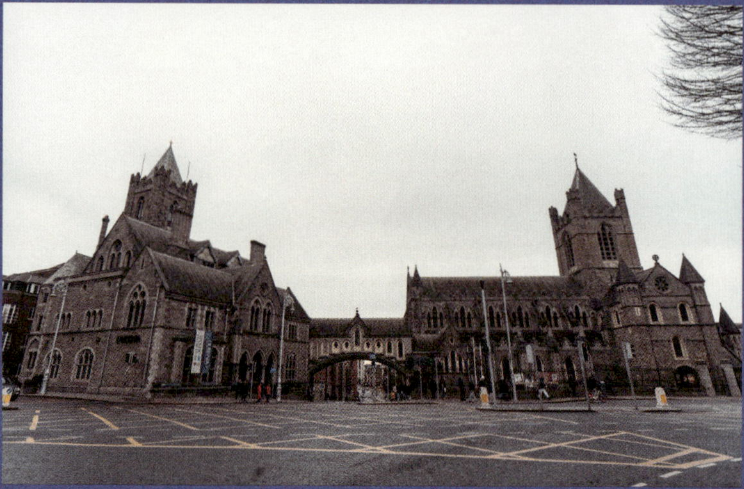

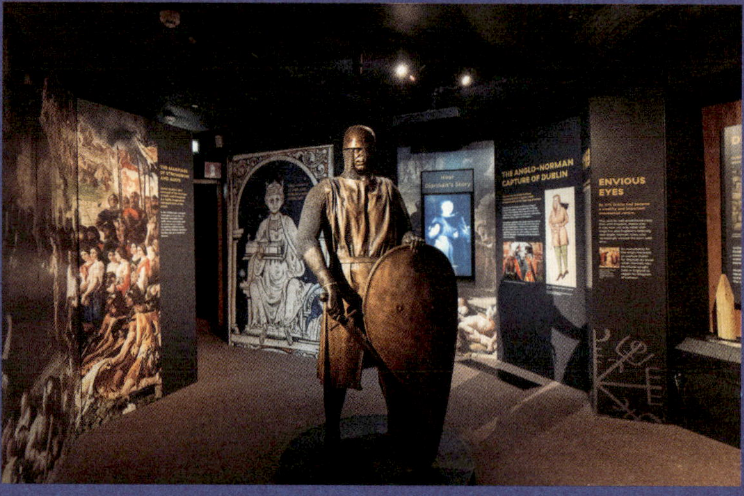
THE ANGLO-NORMAN CAPTURE OF DUBLIN
ENVIOUS EYES

> **66** Step into Medieval Viking Dublin at **Dublinia.** We had a ball experiencing the bustling medieval street, trying on Viking clothing and soaking in the views across the city from St Michael's Tower. **99**

LAURA MAYES, NO FUSS TEAM

DISTILLERY

The Dublin Liberties Distillery 6

Best for:
A peep behind the whiskey curtain.
▪ united.nuns.field

Step inside the Dublin Liberties Distillery and dive into the world of Irish whiskey. Opening its doors in 2019, it blends centuries-old traditions with cutting-edge distilling methods, offering a fascinating look at how their spirits are made. Guided tours take you through the process, from grain to glass, and finish with a tasting of their award-winning whiskeys. No bookings are needed for weekends but if you visit in the week, make sure to secure your spot online beforehand!

EVENTS VENUE

Vicar Street 7

Best for:
Live shows.
▪ hills.even.free

Since opening in 1998, Vicar Street has seen Bob Dylan, Neil Young, Ed Sheeran and Adele play inside its now famous walls. With a maximum capacity of only 1,500, it's an amazing venue for a more intimate experience and to get up close with your favourite artists. It's not just musicians that perform here. Vicar Street pulls in some of the best comedians, drama performances and variety concerts throughout the year. It's definitely worth checking what's on before your trip as tickets can sell out quickly!

ESCAPE ROOM

Incognito Escape Room 8

Best for:
Puzzle solvers.
▪ exams.lance.cigar

Grab your magnifying glass, a notepad and put on your puzzle-solving hat as you tackle an escape room. With over 3,800 five-star reviews on TripAdvisor, it stands as one of Ireland's best-rated escape experiences. Open 7-days a week, you'll need at least two people to take on the rooms, but all ages are welcome (children under 8 and adults over 100 enter for free!). Choose to escape the creepy 'Cabin in the Woods' or channel your inner Sherlock with the 'Baker Street Mystery', just make sure to pre-book your tickets online!

FOOD TOUR

Walking Food Tours 9

Best for:
Foodies & pub lovers.
▪ salsa.reef.fees

Take to the streets and experience the Liberties' culinary scene with Walking Food Tours - (Dublin). The 'Food on Foot' tour takes you on a three-hour journey through the city's best street food spots. Prefer pubs? The 'Drinks on Foot' tour covers traditional pubs over 3.5 hours, sharing brilliant stories about Dublin's drinking traditions. Led by an entertaining guide, these tours are perfect for all ages. Groups can include up to 25 for food tours and 16 for drinks tours, with tickets starting from €25.

DISTILLERY

Roe & Co Distillery

 10

Best for:
Discovering the art of distilling.
■ curry.songs.post

Once extending over 17-acres and the largest exporter of whiskey in Ireland, George Roe & Co. led the way during the 19th-century golden era of whiskey before closing its doors in 1926. Thankfully, in 2017 the distillery was brought back to life under Roe & Co Distillery, with its original windmill tower and a pear tree (which still flowers today) as the last remnants of its former glory. Open 7-days a week, visitors can book on to a variety of activities, from cocktail workshops to whiskey tasting tours.

BREWERY TOUR **EDITORS CHOICE**

Guinness Storehouse

 11

Best for:
Explore the story of Guinness.
■ worker.rate.square

Visitors learn exactly what goes into a pint of the 'black stuff' in this 7-storey brewery. Ending with a complimentary pint in the top floor 'Gravity Bar', whilst enjoying 360-degree views across Dublin. A gift shop and cafés are on-site. Booking is essential. Several tour options are available, including add-ons such as learning how to pour the perfect pint in the 'Guinness Academy Experience' and enjoying an additional pint of Guinness with a picture of your face on top! Did you really go to Dublin without doing the Guinness tour?

DISTILLERY

Pearse Lyons Whiskey Distillery

 12

Best for:
Whiskey & gin enthusiasts.
■ easy.lights.plug

Housed in a beautifully restored 18th-century church, this distillery produces Irish Whiskey and hosts tours and tasting experiences. The distillery first opened in 2017, with the aim of creating 'a distillery like no other in Dublin'. It's not just all whiskey here, guests can enjoy gin workshops. If you're after an uisce beatha experience, you're spoilt for choice, with the tasting and tours on offer. The distillery is open 7-days a week. It's recommended to bring sturdy footwear and suitable outdoor clothing (with some of the tours taking place outside).

THE LIBERTIES & KILMAINHAM

Guinness Storehouse

THE TASTING ROOMS

❝ Did you even visit Dublin if you didn't go to the **Guinness Storehouse?** We'd definitely recommend this iconic attraction. Don't miss the Gravity Bar, where you can enjoy a free pint and 360-views over the city! **❞**

LAURA MAYES, NO FUSS TEAM

MUSEUM

Irish Museum of Modern Art 13

Best for:
Contemporary art lovers.
◼ joke.milk.churn

Found in the stunning 17th-century Royal Hospital Kilmainham, is Ireland's leading contemporary art venue. Known for its cutting-edge exhibitions and fascinating permanent collection, it's a must for art lovers. The lush gardens make for a peaceful wander too. Entry is free for the main exhibits, though special shows may have a small fee. Open Tuesday to Sunday and just a short trip from the city centre, there's also a cosy café for a coffee or some post-museum refuelling with cakes and brownies on offer!

PRISON MUSEUM **EDITORS CHOICE**

Kilmainham Gaol  14

Best for:
Curious history seekers.
◼ drift.bake.shadow

Delve deeper into Dublin's dark past at the famous Kilmainham Gaol. Visitors will discover the stories of people held here as ordinary criminals alongside those who fought for Irish independence. We really enjoyed our visit to Kilmainham and like many other Brits, we were really lacking in knowledge of Irish history. A trip here will certainly provide a great overview of Ireland's major historical events. You'll need to book weeks in advance and the average tour will take around 90 minutes.

MEMORIAL PARK

Irish National War Memorial Park 15

Best for:
Reflection.
◼ exchanges.fleet.broker

The memorial park pays tribute to the 49,400 Irish soldiers who gave their lives during WWI. One of the most famous memorial gardens in Europe, the park includes sunken rose gardens, herbaceous borders and plenty of beautiful trees to admire. Free guided tours are available every Wednesday at 11am from April to October and, if arranged beforehand, visitors can access the book rooms of the memorial where the names of the soldiers can be seen in a beautifully illustrated manuscript.

HISTORICAL CULTURAL CENTRE

Richmond Barracks  16

Best for:
Irish history & culture.
◼ files.goats.closet

Richmond Barracks is a must-visit for history buffs and culture lovers. Once a British Army garrison, it later played a key role in the 1916 Rising, holding over 3,000 prisoners. Today, it's a cultural space with fascinating exhibitions, guided tours and a peaceful garden where dogs are welcome to explore (garden only). You'll discover stories of rebellion, resilience and the site's later life as a school and community hub. Welcoming guests from Monday to Saturday, with only the library open on Mondays.

Kilmainham Gaol

> **66** *Discover the lives of those sentenced to imprisonment at **Kilmainham Gaol**. You'll hear powerful and emotive stories that will stay with you, making this a unique experience that, in my opinion, is a must-see.* **99**

LAURA MAYES, NO FUSS TEAM

WALKING TOUR
THE LIBERTIES

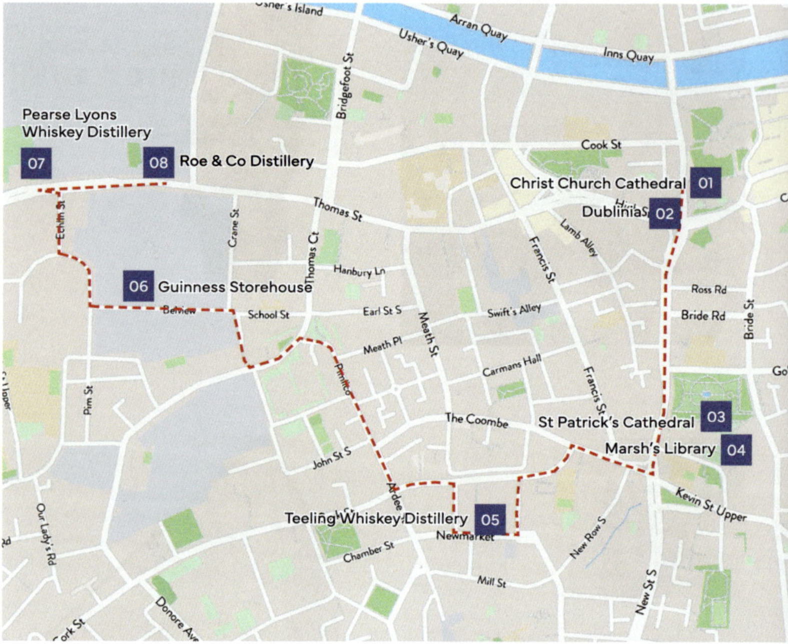

A walk blending history, faith, and flavour! This 3km route weaves through Dublin's cultural heart. Admire the imposing Christ Church Cathedral, steeped in centuries of history, and the architectural beauty of St. Patrick's Cathedral. Pass by bustling markets and cobblestone streets, soaking in the vibrant atmosphere. Whiskey lovers can take a tour at any of the three distilleries now open in this once-thriving whiskey hub!

WALKING TOUR

TOTAL LENGTH: 3KM

DURATION: 40 MINS (NO STOPS)

TERRAIN: RELATIVELY FLAT COBBLES

STARTING POINT: CHRIST CHURCH CATHEDRAL

END POINT: ROE & CO DISTILLERY

01
CHRIST CHURCH CATHEDRAL

06
GUINNESS STOREHOUSE

02
DUBLINIA VIKING MUSEUM

07
PEARSE LYONS WHISKEY DISTILLERY

03
ST PATRICK'S CATHEDRAL

08
ROE & CO DISTILLERY

04
MARSH'S LIBRARY

TIME FOR A BREAK?

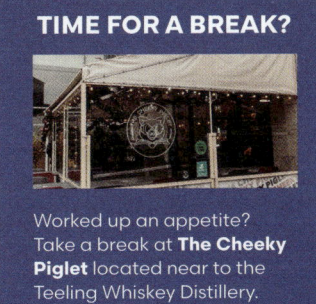

Worked up an appetite? Take a break at **The Cheeky Piglet** located near to the Teeling Whiskey Distillery. Perfect for a coffee and some brunch or lunch.

05
TEELING WHISKEY DISTILLERY

MEMORABLE MOMENT:
A boozy afternoon in the Liberties!

BY NO FUSS TRAVEL EDITOR, LAURA MAYES

We kicked off our morning with some delicious brunch to ensure our stomachs were lined for the day ahead. We ate at Two Pups, the food was fantastic, and we'd highly recommend a visit. Next, we headed to the Teeling Whiskey Distillery for our pre-booked tour. It was an interesting experience learning all about the whiskey production process, followed by a tasting session with neat whiskey and a tasty whiskey-based cocktail—yum! Next on the list was the Guinness Storehouse. For most of our group, this was a second or third visit, but it's somewhere you can visit time and time again and still enjoy! We made our way up the 7-floors *(which became a little crowded at times)* and journeyed through the immersive and impressive displays that showcase the Guinness story. We stopped by the tasting rooms for a guided tasting session *(and a mini-Guinness),* before heading to the 'stoutie' experience to enjoy a pint with our faces on! *(Just a heads up you'll have to pay extra for this experience).* To wrap up our day, we headed to the Gravity Bar on the top floor to enjoy our complimentary pint and watch the sunset over the city – bliss!

> **"** To wrap up our day, we headed to the Gravity Bar on the top floor to enjoy our complimentary pint and watch the sunset over the city – bliss! **"**

ITALIAN   17

Bell Pesto Café Dublin

lofts.life.pepper

Bell Pesto Café serves up fresh Italian flavours in a cosy, laid-back setting. Perfect for breakfast, lunch or a quick coffee, the menu features fresh pasta, paninis and plenty of vegan options. Open Tuesday to Sunday, it's a relaxed spot where you can enjoy authentic Italian bites.

BREWPUB 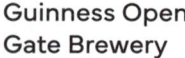   18

Guinness Open Gate Brewery

ranked.resort.plates

Innovation has always been at the heart of Guinness, with its brewers testing and perfecting their creations for over 100 years. A visit here lets you get a peep behind the curtain and taste some of the limited-edition experiments the expert brewers dream up. Closed Tuesday's and Wednesday's.

LOCALS CHOICE

Guinness doesn't just make the black stuff, and there's nowhere better in the world to explore that than the singular **Open Gate**. This previously private staff bar is the brewers' playground is now accessible to the public, serving experimental pints made away from the intoxicating vats of stout. Available here, and only here, is Guinness' take on anything from Witbier to pale ale. A truly special experience.

LOCAL WRITER, JAMES HENDICOTT

Guinness Open Gate

PUB 19

Arthur's Pub

vocal.point.race

Also known as Arthur's Blues and Jazz Club, it's the closest watering hole to the Guinness Storehouse. But it's much more than a convenient stop near one of Dublin's most-visited attractions. Here you'll find a real turf fire (lit everyday), amazing Irish music and plenty of food and drinks to indulge in.

TOASTY SPECIALISTS 20

Griolladh Thomas St

camps.last.oasis

Griolladh serves up gourmet toasties with a twist, using 100% Irish ingredients. From the classic 'Sausage, Egg and Cheese' toastie to non-meat options like the 'Veggie Pudding, Egg and Cheese', there is something for every palate. Overall, an excellent choice for a quick, satisfying bite!

CAFÉ (21)

Oh'Rourke's

saving.chair.drip

If you're after some no-nonsense, affordable Irish breakfast then a trip to Oh'Rourke's along the River Liffey should be on the cards. Expect generous portions, quick service and a warm atmosphere that's perfect for fuelling up before a day of exploring. Oh'Rourke's is closed on Sundays.

PUB (22)

The Brazen Head

stack.basin.bunks

Dating back to 1198, The Brazen Head is said to be Ireland's oldest pub. Enjoy traditional and contemporary live music, wholesome food and maybe even a pint of the black stuff. They're open 7-days a week from 12pm to late, and food is served until 9pm each evening.

MICHELIN-STAR RESTAURANT (23)

Variety Jones

vital.rice.scout

A Michelin-starred gem offering a chef's choice sharing menu brimming with seasonal flavours. Run by brothers Keelan and Aaron Higgs, it pairs inventive dishes with carefully curated wines. With its laid-back atmosphere and top-quality food, it's ideal for a special evening.

CAFÉ (24)

Honest To Goodness Café

diner.select.actors

Offering delicious breakfast and lunch dishes made with fresh, locally sourced Irish produce. Tuck into hearty sandwiches, wholesome salads and daily specials, all prepared in-house. Combine all that with the easy-going atmosphere, and you'll want to return for more!

FINE PUB DINING (25)

Spitalfields

harder.cones.alien

A homely Irish pub with a modern twist, think traditional restaurant cooking in a cosy pub setting. Spitalfields is known for its fresh, hearty dishes and great service. Open Tuesday to Saturday, it's an adults-only spot (no under 16s), perfect for a relaxed evening of food and drinks in style.

The Cheeky Piglet

THE LIBERTIES & KILMAINHAM | WHERE TO EAT & DRINK

CAFÉ

EDITORS CHOICE 26

Two Pups

gums.slower.most

Two Pups is a cosy café serving top-notch coffee, hearty all-day brunches, and plenty of tasty, homemade treats. With its friendly vibe and homely interior, it's a firm local favourite. And, true to its name, a pup or two are more than welcome during your visit!

CAFÉ

 27

Søren & Son

liner.scuba.bless

Is good coffee your thing? Head to Søren & Son, where you can indulge in speciality coffee, within a minimalistic, scandi-inspired setting. They also offer an assortment of delicious pastries and sweet treats to complement your coffee and keep you going!

CAFÉ

LOCALS CHOICE 28

The Fumbally

banana.encounter.surely

The Fumbally prides itself on being an eating and meeting place that cooks food from the heart, baking their own fresh bread and taking coffee seriously. They're open Tuesday - Saturday. You can grab breakfast and lunch here between 8am and 3pm, while hot drinks are served up until 5pm.

BRUNCH

LOCALS CHOICE 29

The Cheeky Piglet

tips.quarrel.unit

The Cheeky Piglet serves all-day brunch featuring favourites like its full Irish breakfast, Vietnamese coffee and loose-leaf teas. With a cosy atmosphere, friendly service and a menu spanning eggs benedict to Kinder Bueno cheesecake and tapioca squares, it's a must-visit!

CAFÉ

 30

Hen's Teeth Dublin

flap.eating.puddles

For those who love great food, art, music and culture, there's no better place to get yourself down to than Hen's Teeth Dublin. As well as hosting all sorts of events, visitors can indulge in out-of-this-world baked goods and coffee from the team at Naked Bites – the on-site café.

LOCALS CHOICE

A rustic, hippie place that serves falafel and kombucha at shared tables, **The Fumbally** is a café, bakery, market, art and events space, and bar; a proper friendly, alternative community that caters to all. Refreshingly healthy and often packed to the rafters, eating here feels like a real local experience, where chatting to strangers is just part of the vibe.

LOCAL WRITER, JAMES HENDICOTT

HOTEL 31

Aloft Dublin City

+353 1 800 409929

term.hood.adults

If fancy hotels aren't your bag, Aloft offers plenty of fun mixed in with convenience and comfort. From family rooms with tent beds for little ones to a robot butler delivering room service, the whole family (including dogs!) will love their stay here.

HOTEL 32

Premier Inn Dublin The Liberties Hotel

+353 1 263 5319

mugs.sulk.sticky

Comfy beds, 'power showers' and a convenient location are the big selling points for the Liberties' Premier Inn. Just a short walk from many of the area's main attractions, it's a budget-friendly choice combining affordability with modern amenities.

HOTEL 33

Hyatt Centric The Liberties Dublin

+353 1 708 1999

speak.start.noting

The 4-star Hyatt Centric combines sleek rooms, a cosy bar and delicious dining with a 24-hour gym (which must be pre-booked). Ideal for a relaxing and stylish stay, it's a great spot if you fancy treating yourself during your Dublin trip!

HOSTEL 34

Canbe Garden Lane Backpackers Hostel

+353 1 551 5733

cost.discouraged.fries

Canbe Garden Lane Backpackers Hostel is a friendly option for budget travellers, offering shared dorms (including female-only options) and private rooms. Guests can also enjoy a complimentary continental breakfast each morning!

APARTHOTEL 35

Staycity Aparthotels Dublin Tivoli

+353 1 556 7890

waddled.rabble.stale

Offering one-bedroom and studio apartments, Staycity Aparthotels provide all the comforts of home life with the convenience of a hotel, including fully equipped kitchens, 24-hour reception, a laundry room and an on-site gym.

HOTEL 36

Hilton Dublin Kilmainham

+353 1 420 1800

warns.sober.garage

The Hilton Dublin Kilmainham is a 4-star hotel offering 130 modern rooms, a bar, restaurant with terrace and a health club – including a pool! It's conveniently located near Kilmainham Gaol and the Irish Museum of Modern Art.

Staycity Aparthotels Dublin Tivoli

Temple Bar

Dublin's most iconic spot, Temple Bar, is packed with buzzing pubs, vibrant eateries, and quirky boutiques. It's the place to be if you want to soak up the lively atmosphere, and with plenty of hotels nearby, it's ideal for a quick city getaway.

PAGES 118 - 137

TEMPLE BAR:
Best for a pint of the black stuff, trad music and culture.

Dublin's best-known district, Temple Bar, is filled with pubs, boutiques, eateries, and more. Wander the cobbled streets to explore the street murals of the Icon Walk, catch a performance at the Olympia Theatre, or visit the Temple Bar Food Market (open every Saturday). It's a busy, crowded tourist hotspot, so make sure to keep your belongings close by. You'll pay a premium for food and drinks in this area, but it's a must-visit for anyone exploring Dublin to experience the buzz, day and night. You'll also find traditional music in most pubs in the area.

TOP 5 THINGS TO SEE & DO

01
THE TEMPLE BAR PUB

02
WORLD OF ILLUSION

03
HA'PENNY BRIDGE

04
PHOTO MUSEUM IRELAND

05
IRISH ROCK 'N' ROLL MUSEUM

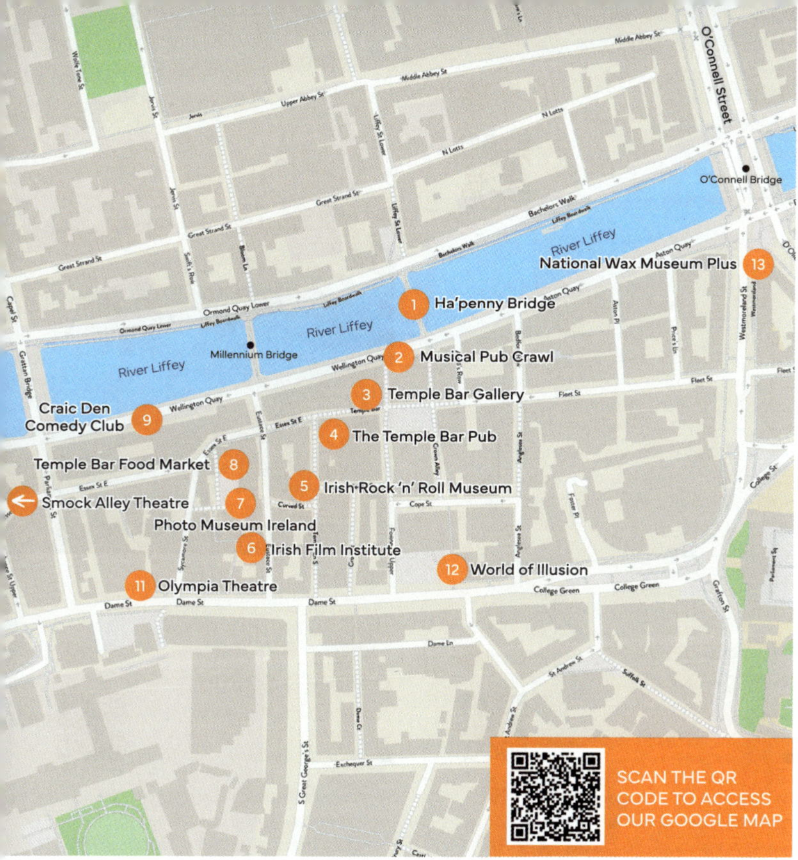

GETTING HERE

🚶 **Approx. Walking Distance From: Temple Bar**
O'Connell St (10 mins), Smithfield (16 mins), The Liberties (15 mins), St Stephen's Green (19 mins), Merrion Square (23 mins), Grand Canal Dock (26 mins)

🚋 **Luas Tram: Green Line**
Stop: Westmoreland (5 min walk)

🚌 **Bus Routes to Temple Bar: 130, 14, 26, 27, 39A, 46A, 69, 783**
Stops: Dublin Halfpenny Bridge, Dame Street, Temple Bar, Wellington Quay, Crampton Quay, Aston Quay

HISTORIC ATTRACTION

Ha'penny Bridge

Best for:
Riverside views.
number.camera.saying

Located a few minutes' walk from Temple Bar, this historic cast-iron bridge resides over the River Liffey and goes by the official name, The Liffey Bridge. Built in 1816, it was the first pedestrian bridge to span the River Liffey and used to cost ha'penny to cross (hence the name Ha'penny Bridge). It's worth a short stop to look at this 'old- world Dublin attraction' or use it on your route to get from one side of the river to the other (it's said that around 30,000 people cross each day).

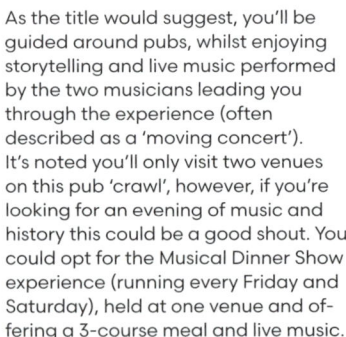

Ha'penny Bridge

LIVE MUSIC

Musical Pub Crawl

Best for:
Live music & history.
fall.toned.august

As the title would suggest, you'll be guided around pubs, whilst enjoying storytelling and live music performed by the two musicians leading you through the experience (often described as a 'moving concert'). It's noted you'll only visit two venues on this pub 'crawl', however, if you're looking for an evening of music and history this could be a good shout. You could opt for the Musical Dinner Show experience (running every Friday and Saturday), held at one venue and offering a 3-course meal and live music.

ART GALLERY

Temple Bar Gallery & Studios

Best for:
Contemporary art enthusiasts.
tracks.closet.amount

A must-visit for contemporary art enthusiasts, or those looking for a budget-friendly activity. Established by artists in 1983, the space focuses on creating an inclusive environment and is comprised of 30 studios, providing a place for artists to thrive and visitors to experience contemporary art. For free. The free public events also allow visitors to meet artists, get inside the studios, ask questions, make their own art and learn something new through workshops, talks, screenings and tours.

ICONIC PUB

The Temple Bar Pub

Best for:
A pint of the black stuff.
doctor.yards.good

The hallmark of the Temple Bar district, dating back to 1840. This iconic venue hosts traditional Irish music sessions every day, showcasing a fine sample of talented musicians from around the country, and is home to Ireland's largest whiskey collection. You'll pay a premium for food and drinks here, which is to be expected due to the pub's legendary status. Even if you decide not to head inside, you must pay a visit just to grab a photo outside this iconic spot and soak in the friendly atmosphere!

MUSEUM **EDITORS CHOICE**

The Irish Rock 'N' Roll Museum Experience

Best for:
Wannabe rock stars.
slate.safety.values

Follow in the footsteps of legends like Thin Lizzy and get a peep behind the curtain of one of Dublin's top music venues and recording studios with a trip to the Irish Rock 'N' Roll Museum Experience. Part museum, part studio session, here you'll find official memorabilia from some of Ireland's biggest artists. We appreciated the fine delivery of this tour; the guide's passion was infectious. Open all week, each tour takes just over an hour, with the first starting at 10.30am and the last at 5pm.

CINEMA

Irish Film Institute

Best for:
Film & culture enthusiasts.
ages.jobs.cracks

The Irish Film Institute, originally founded in 1943, is a hub for film lovers and a key institution for preserving Ireland's cinematic legacy. The venue features a multi-screen cinema, café bar, shop, beer garden, and library. While this hip hangout specialises in arty and independent films, be sure to take a look at 'What's On' during your trip. You might just recognise one or two of the films being shown, and let's face it: there's no better way to escape the temperamental Dublin weather.

MUSEUM

Photo Museum Ireland

Best for:
Art & culture enthusiasts.
decent.shirts.mint

This award-winning gallery, established in 1978, is considered Ireland's national centre for contemporary photography. So, it goes without saying, this is must-visit for keen photographers and admirers of photography. The space is comprised of exhibition spaces, a specialist photography bookshop and artist production facilities. You could visit one of their free exhibitions, free guided tours (available on weekday evenings and weekends), or a paid workshop. Book ahead online.

TEMPLE BAR

MARKET

Temple Bar Food Market

Best for:
Locally sourced Irish produce.

assure.lift.handed

A little slice of foodie heaven! The Temple Bar Food Market was established in 1997 by a group of Irish farmers and producers and is one of Dublin's oldest and longest running outdoor food markets. The market still features many of the original traders, with stalls taking over Meeting House Square every Saturday (from 10am-4.30pm) and offering up local, artisan and high-quality Irish produce – from farmhouse cheese wheels to freshly baked sourdough sandwiches.

COMEDY CLUB — EDITORS CHOICE

Craic Den Comedy Club

Best for:
Comedy lovers.

modern.ocean.reject

Renowned for its vibrant atmosphere and top-tier comedy line-ups, Craic Den, located in the heart of Temple Bar at The Workman's Club, hosts comedy 7-nights a week. *(It's also a great spot for live music).* This intimate venue is the perfect setting for some raucous Irish comedy. The Craic Den is a fantastic addition to your Dublin night out. Expect epic, Guinness-fuelled crowd interactions that the acts thrive on. Tickets range in price from €10 to €15, offering superb value. We highly recommend!

THEATRE

Smock Alley Theatre

Best for:
Theatre, dance & comedy lovers.

blend.fries.spoke

Theatre lovers rejoice! Spend an evening enjoying live music, theatre and comedy at this restored 17th century theatre, situated on the banks of the River Liffey. Smock Alley Theatre, labelled Ireland's 'oldest, newest theatre', was the first custom built theatre in Dublin City. Originally built in 1662, the theatre reopened its doors in May 2012, following a 6-year renovation, to once again become a bustling hub of theatre, dance, music, comedy and visual arts. Visit their website to book tickets.

THEATRE

Olympia Theatre

Best for:
Live entertainment.

twig.dates.runner

Dublin's Olympia Theatre dates back to the late 19th century and has hosted all sorts of acts – from legends like Charlie Chaplin, to iconic bands such as Radiohead and the Foo Fighters, and many others. It's not just musicians that grace its stage, you can catch pantomimes, stand up acts, dramas and live podcast shows, to name just a few! With a capacity of up to 1,600, shows here strike the perfect balance between big productions and the intimacy often lost in larger venues.

LOCALS CHOICE

"In a sensational music scene, the gorgeous old **Olympia Theatre** might be the best venue. Typically hosting rock, pop, and indie, it's worth getting in here for anything to see its decorative design."

LOCAL WRITER, JAMES HENDICOTT

OPTICAL ILLUSIONS

World of Illusion

12

Best for:
Mind-bending adventures.
■ digits.stones.ranks

Step into a world of mind-bending illusions, gravity-defying rooms and out-of-this-world light displays with a visit to World of Illusion. Enjoy interactive exhibits where reality makes way for magic, including infinity mirrors, a vortex tunnel that will have you spinning, a giant kaleidoscope for photo opportunities and perspective illusions to challenge what is real and what isn't. Open daily, grab your tickets online and allow for around an hour to explore all 3 floors of this mind-melting attraction.

MUSEUM

The National Wax Museum Plus

13

Best for:
Family-friendly fun.
■ cherry.useful.runs

If you're looking for something fun to do with the kids, or perhaps a rainy-day activity, head here. This unique and interactive museum is suitable for all ages and there's plenty to see, with three floors to explore. Journey through Irish history, heritage, and popular culture throughout sections such as the Science and Discovery room, the Enchanted Forest, Mirror Maze, and, if you're brave enough, the Chamber of Horrors! There's also the option to take on a Murder Mystery tour (guided or self-guided).

TEMPLE BAR

World of Illusion

WALKING TOUR
TEMPLE BAR

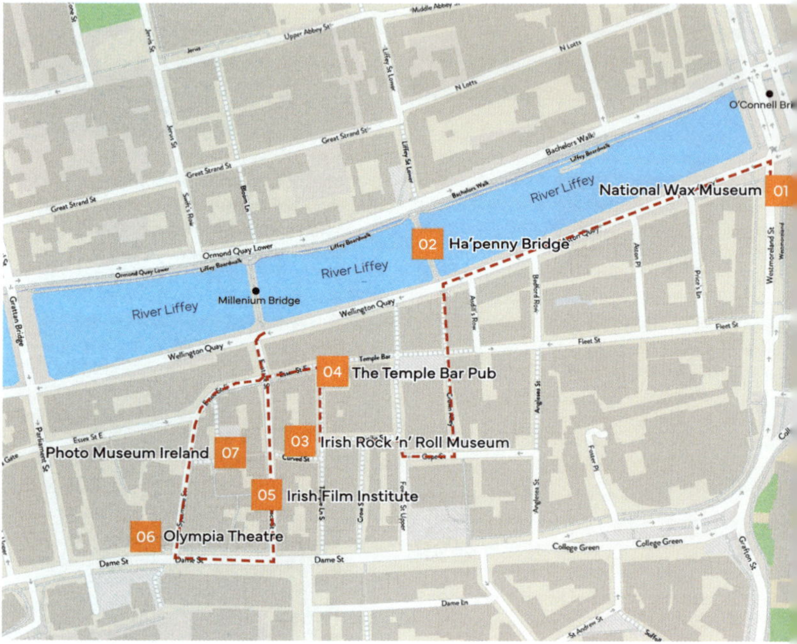

A short and winding stroll through the cobbled backstreets of Temple Bar, where you'll soak up the infectious Dublin atmosphere. Along the way, you'll pass the iconic Ha'penny Bridge, head through Merchant's Arch, and see many of Temple Bar's legendary spots. This could easily be turned into a mini pub crawl, with stops at The Old Storehouse, The Temple Bar, The Norseman, and The Wild Duck!

WALKING TOUR

TOTAL LENGTH: 1.3KM

DURATION: 20 MINS (NO STOPS)

TERRAIN: COBBLED PAVEMENT

STARTING POINT: THE WAX MUSEUM

END POINT: MILLENIUM BRIDGE

01
THE NATIONAL WAX MUSEUM PLUS

06
OLYMPIA THEATRE

02
HA'PENNY BRIDGE

07
PHOTO MUSEUM IRELAND

03
IRISH ROCK 'N' ROLL MUSEUM

04
THE TEMPLE BAR

05
IRISH FILM INSTITUTE

TIME FOR A BREAK?

Worked up a thirst? Take a break at **The Old Storehouse Bar & Restaurant** where live music, cold pints and delicious bites are almost guaranteed!

TEMPLE BAR

MEMORABLE MOMENT:
The magic of Temple Bar!

BY NO FUSS TRAVEL EDITOR, ROB STANDLEY

On our most recent trip to Dublin, we spent the morning exploring The Liberties before heading to Temple Bar, the city's beating heart and a place I have a huge soft spot for. The cost of a pint here can be eye-watering, but if you overlook that, you'll become fully immersed in everything that makes Dublin great. On this particular trip, we were delighted to meet with our good friends Kellie and Cillian, who had made the journey up from Cork.

Our first group activity was a light-hearted 'murder mystery' experience at the National Wax Museum Plus, which we failed miserably at. The museum itself is like most wax museums I've visited before—nothing incredible to write home about, but a solid rainy-day jaunt *(especially if you're travelling with kids)*. After a quick pint at The Old Storehouse in Temple Bar *(one of many iconic pubs where live traditional music is almost guaranteed)*, we made the short walk to Bobo's Burgers. This place was a wee bit more sophisticated than a typical burger joint. The food was superb and definitely hit the spot after a few pints!

> **❝** There's something truly magical about Temple Bar. It has an aura, a charm that's really hard to put into words. **❞**

We ended the night at the Craic Den Comedy Club, which was absolutely worth the €15 ticket. The comedians were on top form and really fed off the Guinness-fuelled interactions with the punters. Don't be put off by the unusual venue—it feels like you're in someone's living room, but that only adds to the intimate atmosphere.

There's something truly magical about Temple Bar. It has an aura, a charm that's really hard to put into words... Once you stumble through the doors of one of its wholesome pubs, perhaps you'll feel the same...

PUB   14

Darkey Kelly's

games.pitch.option

A traditional, comforting pub with an old-school feel to it. The place to head if you're looking to enjoy some traditional live music, performed by local musicians 7-nights a week! They also offer some hearty food. Please note they do not take bookings, it's walk-ins only.

BAKERY   15

il Valentino Bakery & Café

cargo.tools.moves

Authentic European bakes and coffee, sound good? Head to il Valentino. Formerly known as the highly endorsed 'Queen of Tarts', this bakery (ran by French chef Morgan Gela) pride themselves in only offering products baked from scratch, daily, in their own bakery, using an artisan approach.

LGBTQIA+ BAR   16

Street 66

exact.relay.vibrates

Street 66 is an LGBTQIA+ friendly bar with funky décor, an extensive gin menu and live DJ nights playing classic tunes. Known for its inclusive and welcoming atmosphere, it's a great spot for a fun and memorable night. They're open every night, ideal if you fancy an evening cocktail or two.

JAPANESE 17

DARUMA

quiz.among.fuzzy

Looking for a casual yet vibrant dining spot? Head to DARUMA to enjoy some authentic Japanese food. They specialise in sake cocktails, wagyu beef and small plates, which are designed to share between friends (although, in our opinion, there's nothing wrong with having them all to yourself!).

PUB   18

Porterhouse Temple Bar

race.thinks.wires

Live music, home-brewed beer and a warm and inviting atmosphere, what more could you want? They were Ireland's first pub brewery (opening in 1996) and today offer a choice of exclusive brews. If you're partial to a pint of the black stuff, why not give the Porterhouse Stout a try!

Tula Mexican Grill

BURGERS 19

WOWBURGER
Temple Bar

spoil.that.museum

WOWBURGER takes its craft seriously – the team spent months creating the perfect patty, sourcing freshly baked buns and settling on seasonal potatoes for its fries. Choose from a reasonably priced menu that covers all the burger basics. You'll find them inside the Giddy Dolphin pub.

Café 20

Joy of
Chá

hike.values.ending

This gastro café is Dublin's first speciality tea shop, offering premium teas, coffees and hot chocolate! They also offer a variety of food options including all day breakfast (from a traditional Irish breakfast to loaded breakfast nachos) and homemade cakes. They're usually open everyday from 9am – 8.30pm.

MEXICAN 21

Tula Mexican
Grill

silver.patrol.grand

Fresh, fast and delicious burritos, bowls, tacos and salads. If Mexican is a firm favourite of yours, you need to try this place! They pride themselves on using the finest ingredients, with salsas and guacamole made fresh every day. Fancy a midnight burrito? They're open until 4am on weekends.

Bunsen

BURGERS 22

Bunsen
Temple Bar

gallons.less.liner

Offering burgers, fries and creamy shakes, the menu might be small and simple, but the burgers are mighty! Both the burgers and buns are freshly made (by hand) every morning. Bunsen was opened by two cousins in 2013, and today they run multiple locations in Dublin, Cork and Belfast.

131

TEMPLE BAR | WHERE TO EAT & DRINK

PUB (23)
The Norseman
decent.chief.palace

Beer, whiskey, food and music... according to The Norseman (previously named Farringtons), these four words sum up what they're about! Relax and soak up the atmosphere, with live music on offer 7-days a week! They also have five en-suite bedrooms if you're looking for somewhere to stay.

RESTAURANT & BAR (24)
The Quays
lucky.lock.arrive

Another traditional pub with good beer and live music on offer daily. You'll find the restaurant upstairs, specialising in traditional Irish dishes like Guinness stew, Wicklow lamb shank and Dublin coddle. There are separate menus for gluten free and vegetarian options.

RESTAURANT & BAR (25)
Merchant's Arch
combining.joke.ruled

Located beside the famous Ha'penny Bridge, you'll find the bar downstairs (offering live music every evening) and the restaurant upstairs. The ideal stop if you're looking for a bite to eat at any point in the day, they offer everything from a breakfast menu, to light bites to a filling three-course meal.

JAPANESE & SUSHI (26)
Banyi Japanese Dining
wires.bleat.beard

Fancy escaping the busy pubs and live music for something a little different? Head to Banyi to enjoy some authentic and affordable Japanese dishes, including fresh sashimi, hand-crafted sushi, noodles, rice bowls, bento boxes, gyozas... you'll be spoilt for choice!

The Norseman

PUB 27

The Auld Dubliner

■ love.buzz.audit

Situated in the very heart of Temple Bar, The Auld Dubliner is another spot with a lively atmosphere – offering daily live music and authentic Irish food (like beef & Guinness casserole). They also have six en-suite bedrooms if you're looking for somewhere to stay.

RESTAURANT & BAR 28

Oliver St. John Gogarty

■ tigers.school.launch

Enjoy three floors of olde world charm, set across two of the oldest buildings in the Temple Bar Quarter. There's a bar, beer garden, music hall (with live traditional music sessions every day from 1pm to 2am!) and an award-winning restaurant offering traditional Irish food.

BAR & WHISKEY MERCHANTS 29

The Palace Bar

■ voters.hops.caked

The appeal of this family-run bar starts on the street, with its facade adorned in flowers. Dating back to 1823, The Palace is one of the oldest pubs in Dublin. Head upstairs and you'll find the dedicated whiskey bar and store – known as the 'Whiskey Palace'.

FINE DINING 30

D'Olier Street Restaurant

■ brick.upon.cheeks

Michelin-starred and serving a 13-course seasonal tasting menu. It might be 'fine dining', but this eatery's motto – "It's not fancy, it's fun" – means everyone's welcome. Make sure to book in advance and if you're an aspiring chef, grab a seat at the chef's counter for a front-row view of the culinary wizardry!

PUB **LOCALS CHOICE** 31

Mulligan's

■ blitz.saving.laws

A great stop for a pint of the black stuff! Mulligan's is known for its colourful history (beginning as an unlicensed drinking venue, before serving pints legally in 1782). It's old-school interior and links to reported ghost sightings make for a unique experience.

RESTAURANT & BAR 32

The Old Storehouse

■ begins.that.couch

Celebrated for its live music (7-days a week) and lively atmosphere! Depending on what you're after they have several areas to choose from… an intimate snug bar, a lively main bar, a venue bar and two heated beer gardens. Food is served daily from 12pm - 9pm.

EATERY (33)

Mongolian Barbeque

◼ found.forum.most

Noted to be serving the 'freshest stir fry in Dublin', Mongolian Barbeque offers a relaxed atmosphere and a dining experience with a difference. Choose from a selection of seafood, meat, tofu, noodles and vegetables, and watch the grillers cook fresh in front of you.

EATERY (34)

Rosa Madre

◼ rents.damage.ropes

An authentic, Italian style seafood restaurant. Not a seafood lover? Don't worry, there's a selection of pasta dishes and vegetarian options available. It's quite the hotspot for celebrities, you might recognise some of the famous faces that have dined there on their Instagram (@rosamadredublin).

EATERY (35)

Il Vicoletto

◼ noisy.horn.soccer

Looking for a fine-dining option? Il Vicoletto offers traditional Central-Northern Italian cuisine within an intimate setting. They use local produce, as well as importing cheeses, oils and boutique wines straight from Italy. We'd recommend one of their handmade pasta dishes.

STEAKHOUSE — LOCALS CHOICE (36)

FX Buckley Steakhouse (Crow St)

◼ stress.libraries.nasal

A haven for meat-lovers, FX Buckley Steakhouse brings decades worth of experience in sourcing and serving the finest cuts of meat. Its signature dry-aged steaks are cooked to perfection, while the dark wooded interior makes for a cosy and comfortable set up to savour every bite!

BURGERS — EDITORS CHOICE (37)

BóBós Burgers

◼ target.hunt.exile

Offering "Dublin's finest" gourmet Irish burgers since 2006. The ideal place for a top-notch burger, or a group with mixed food preferences, as they offer, beef, chicken, veggie and vegan options! They also offer a selection of breakfast and dessert options. We loved this place!

PUB (38)

Foggy Dew

◼ fetch.taking.varieties

Established in 1901, this historical pub is the perfect place to stop for a pint or two, or if you're looking for somewhere a little less lively – with live music usually performed twice a week (rather than 7-days a week like most pubs within the Temple Bar area).

BóBós Burgers

HOTEL 39

Harding Hotel

+353 1 679 6500

■ stand.look.sizes

This cosy hotel is located inside a historic Victorian building that sits on the very edge of Temple Bar (on Fishamble Street). It's only an approx. 3-minute walk from Dublin Castle and Christ Church Cathedral, a great place to stay if you want to be central.

HOTEL 40

NYX Hotel Dublin Christchurch

+353 1 482 5000

■ noises.upgrading.cage

Looking for a chic place to relax and unwind after a busy day of exploring? You'll find this hotel nestled between the bustling Temple Bar and vibrant Liberties districts. They have an equally as elegant on-site bar and restaurant.

The Morgan Hotel

HOTEL 41

The Clarence Hotel

+353 1 407 0800

■ washed.whites.cans

A luxury, boutique hotel, offering views over the River Liffey. This place is somewhat of an icon, dating back to 1852. It's also known as the 'U2 Hotel' or 'Bono Hotel', as it was previously owned by the musician himself. There's also on-site dining options here.

HOTEL 42

The Morgan Hotel

+353 1 643 7000

■ lakes.focal.combining

Enjoy a comfortable stay at this 4-star hotel, with an in-house bar and restaurant. Travelling with your dog? They offer a super dog- friendly stay (for 1 small/medium dog under 20kg), including welcome treats, bowls, a floor mat and a bed.

HOTEL 43

Temple Bar Hotel

+353 1 677 3333

■ scan.head.spring

The aptly named Temple Bar Hotel is located within a prime city-centre location, just a 3-minute stroll from the famous Temple Bar Pub. They offer everything from pod rooms to executive king suites. Book direct and get a complimentary cocktail on arrival.

The Fleet Hotel

HOTEL

The Fleet Hotel

+353 1 670 8124

final.vast.grace

As the name suggests, this elegant hotel is situated on Fleet Street. Once home to one of Europe's finest tea houses (Bewley's Café), today its home to stylish accommodation and an on-site bar, café and outdoor terrace.

HOTEL

Temple Bar Inn

+353 1 484 5010

jaws.jolly.decreased

Situated across the street from the Palace Bar, this vibrant hotel is in an ideal spot to be immersed within this bustling district. There's an on-site restaurant and bar, complete with pool table and live sport showings. Save money by booking direct.

Grafton Street, St Stephen's Green & Portobello

St. Stephen's Green is perfect for a leisurely stroll, whilst Grafton Street is full of shops, cafés, eateries and street performers. With so many must-see spots and hotels nearby, it's a great place to explore and stay.

GRAFTON STREET, ST STEPHEN'S GREEN & PORTOBELLO:
Eat, explore & stay.

For those craving a mix of history, scenic walks and cosy corners to unwind in after a day of exploration, Dublin's Grafton Street, Stephen's Green & Portobello district offers all that and more. Head to Grafton Street to enjoy some of the city's finest street performers and inviting cafés, ideal for a lazy afternoon of people watching and sipping good coffee. Just steps away, St Stephen's Green and its lush greenery awaits for a peaceful escape from the city's busy streets. Finally, head over to Portobello, with its vintage shops, live music scene and pubs brimming with Irish charm and craic to complete the perfect 'Dublin Day!'.

TOP 5 THINGS TO SEE & DO

01
TRINITY COLLEGE & THE BOOK OF KELLS

02
DUBLIN CASTLE

03
CHESTER BEATTY LIBRARY

04
ST STEPHEN'S GREEN

05
GEORGE'S STREET ARCADE

GETTING HERE

Approx. Walking Distance From: St Stephens Green
O'Connell St (15 mins), Smithfield (33 mins), The Liberties (25 mins), Temple Bar (19 mins), Merrion Square (14 mins), Grand Canal Dock (29 mins)

Luas Tram: Green Line
Stops: Trinity & St Stephens Green

Bus Routes to Grafton Street & St Stephen's Green: 14, 145, 37, 46A, 65
Stops: College Green, Stephen's Green North, Stephen's Green, Stephen's Court, Stephen's Green East, Earlsfort Terrace, Dawson Street

THEATRE

Samuel Beckett Theatre

Best for:
Local theatre productions.
reduce.lions.placed

Opened in 1992 and named after one of the most important playwrights of the 20th century, the Samuel Beckett Theatre is a must-visit for all stage lovers. Found within Trinity College, during term time the theatre showcases the work of students before welcoming touring productions during the holidays. Festivals also take place here throughout the year from the Dublin Dance Festival to the Fringe Festival, so it's well worth checking to see if your trip aligns with any of these events so you can grab tickets in advance!

HISTORIC **EDITORS CHOICE**

Trinity College & The Book of Kells

Best for:
Exploring Dublin's history.
bother.doll.cover

Founded in 1592, Trinity College is Ireland's most prestigious university and attracts more than two million visitors every year. It's home to a set of Georgian and Victorian buildings, cobbled squares and wildflower meadows which all make for an elegant and pleasant place to wander around. Its biggest draw for visitors is the barrel-vaulted Long Room in the Old Library and the Book of Kells; a Gospel manuscript that dates back to the 9th century. Booking in advance is ideal, entry prices vary.

MUSEUM

Irish Whiskey Museum

Best for:
Irish whiskey history & tasting!
gossip.pilots.badge

Discover the story of Irish whiskey through guided tours and tasting. Independent of all whiskey distilleries, The Irish Whiskey Museum offers its visitors the opportunity to taste and experience a huge selection of Irish Whiskey. Different tour types are available, the classic tour will take around an hour, or you could upgrade to the premium tour *(where you'll get to keep your glass)*, or a blending experience *(where you'll take home a small bottle of your own blend)*. Pre-book tickets online.

STATUE

Molly Malone Statue

Best for:
A quick photo opportunity.
caves.wisdom.limbs

Located in the heart of the city's historic Georgian Quarter is the statue of Molly Malone. Known as a little Irish folklore, as there's no concrete evidence that Molly really existed, the story says that she lived a 'double life' as a fishmonger and a woman of the night (hence why Dubliners gave her the nickname the 'The Tart with the Cart'). Today she's the star of the well-known 'Cockles and Mussels' Irish ballad and photos of the statue can often be found on postcards and other Dublin souvenirs.

Trinity College & The Book of Kells

> **Trinity College & The Book of Kells** is a must-visit! I especially enjoyed the second part of the exhibition, which made you feel fully immersed within the story - emotive and brilliant!

LAURA MAYES, NO FUSS TEAM

BUS TOUR — EDITORS CHOICE

The Gravedigger Ghost Bus Tour

5

Best for: Discovering Dublin's spooky side.

last.behave.island

Have you ever wondered what it would be like to wander the eerie streets of Dublin some 600 years ago as the plague took hold of the city? Bit of a weird desire (no judgement here) but this bus tour has you covered! Departing from the College Green bus stop at 7:45pm, the brilliant guides take you to three spooky locations to regale the horrors of Dublin, including a haunted church and a former prison. Not for the faint hearted, the two-hour tour is suggested for those 14 years or older.

CASTLE

Dublin Castle

6

Best for: Castle tours & scenic gardens.

couches.gross.watch

There's lots to explore at Dublin Castle, including its complex history, underground tunnels, the Chapel Royal and it's Medieval Tower. Exploring the scenic castle gardens is said to be one of the best 'free' things to do in Dublin. If you want to discover more inside this unique looking castle, then you'll need to purchase entrance tickets. Self-guided tickets cost €8 for adults and €4 for children (under 12's go free). Guided tours are available for an additional charge. There is a café and gift shop on site.

MUSEUM

Chester Beatty Library

7

Best for: Learning about cultures around the world.

dome.dated.hints

Coined by many visitors as a *'cultural treasure'* and a *'highly recommended visit'*, the Chester Beatty allows its guests to learn about cultures from around the globe. Take a journey across continents and countries, through engaging exhibits with drawings, manuscripts and paintings on show. Open across the week, apart from Mondays between November and March, entry is free, although there's a suggested donation of €10. There's an on-site shop and café, if you fancy a bite to eat.

The Gravedigger Ghost Bus Tour

SHOPPING

George's Street Arcade

⑧

Best for:
Independent shops & eateries.
🔲 soup.soccer.void

A treasure trove of independent and unique stores, eateries and even an art gallery, George's Street Arcade has been the home of over 40 independent retailers since opening in 1881. This Victorian market, housed within a beautiful red-brick building, was Ireland's first purpose-built shopping centre, and one of Europe's oldest city markets. From vintage clothes and books, to baked goods and burgers, this small but bustling market has it all. It's open every day, but opening times vary.

Dublin Castle

WORKSHOP   EDITORS CHOICE

Silver Works Jewellery Making

⑨

Best for:
Learning a new skill.
🔲 email.resort.hidden

If you're looking for a unique activity during your trip to Dublin, book onto a workshop at Silver Works, an award-winning jewellery experience. Guided by some of the best jewellers in Ireland, you'll learn the basics of silver-smithing and walk out with a one-of-a-kind homemade piece of jewellery. The most popular workshop is the 'Forge a Silver Ring' programme which runs 7-days a week across two locations. If rings aren't your thing, there are also silver charm classes and metal clay necklace workshops.

TOUR

Dublin Literary Pub Crawl

⑩

Best for:
Learning about Irish writers.
🔲 corn.souk.degree

Not like your average pub tour, this one takes its guests from one historic watering hole to the next while actors perform the works of some of Dublin's most famous writers. Combining street theatre with the craic that makes the city's pubs some of the very best in the world, we can say with assurance that you don't want to miss this tour. Running nightly from April to October and then Thursday to Sunday evenings from November to late March, tickets need to be purchased in advance.

> **"** History and art fans will appreciate a visit to **Dublin Castle.** Be sure to visit the Dubh Linn Garden located behind the castle, where you'll also discover the Chester Beatty Library. **"**

LAURA MAYES, NO FUSS TEAM

GRAFTON STREET, ST STEPHEN'S GREEN & PORTOBELLO

THEATRE

Gaiety Theatre 11

Best for:
Diverse theatre productions.
arch.punks.claims

This theatre has entertained Dubliners through two world wars, its fight for independence and plenty more of the nation's other ups and downs since its grand opening in 1871. From operas to musicals to comedies, it's known for its diverse touring productions. The interior of the theatre is worth paying for alone, with its Victorian-era design – plush red seating, grand chandelier and viewing on three levels. If you haven't booked tickets in advance, keep in mind the on-site Box Office is cashless.

PUBLIC PARK

St Stephen's Green 12

Best for:
Escaping the city.
radio.hood.supper

Despite being in the centre of Dublin's main shopping district, this public park, that opened its gates in 1880, feels miles away from the nearby busy streets. The park has been maintained to keep its original Victorian layout with 750 trees and extensive plants. Visitors can wander through two miles of accessible pathways, passing a waterfall, an ornamental lake and a children's playground. Keep in mind the park closes according to daylight hours so for winter visits, pop by earlier!

CITY TOUR

Viking Splash Tours 13

Best for:
A unique view of Dublin.
atom.using.next

Explore Dublin like never before across both land and water aboard this tour. With the help of an expert guide, you'll dive deep into the history and culture of the city as well as literally dive into the Grand Canal basin for a cruise along the river. Using an authentic WWII amphibious vehicle, with a Viking theme make-over (including Viking hats for those aboard!), the tour lasts just over an hour and departs from St Stephen's Green. You'll need to book your tickets in advance, concessions available.

BUS TOUR

Vintage Tea Trips 14

Best for:
Tea tasting and a history lesson.
copper.ticket.recall

Enjoy afternoon tea the Irish way. Step onto a vintage 1960s bus and travel back to a time when tea and good conversation were Dublin's main form of entertainment. Sit back, sip on some tea (Barry's, of course) and enjoy some sweet treats as the guides tell tales of Dublin that won't be found in any history book. The tour takes guests past many of the city's famous landmarks so it's a great option if you're pressed for time on your trip. Discounted tickets are available for children.

MUSEUM

Museum of Literature Ireland

Best for:
Lovers of Irish literature.
brick.laser.shells

Whether you're an Irish literature aficionado or a total beginner, you'll be sure to leave the MoLI inspired. The museum celebrates the very best of Irish poets, playwrights and novelists through interactive exhibitions. Open 7-days a week, the MoLI is actually housed in the very building where James Joyce studied. If learning about Ireland's great writers leaves you craving a reading session, head out to the Readers Garden, where you'll find a few cosy spots to dive into a good book!

CYCLING TOUR

Cycle Dublin Bike & E-Bike Tours

Best for:
Discovering Dublin on two wheels.
noting.dozed.pillow

Weaving through Dublin's canals, whizzing past its most famed landmarks and winding by the many Georgian Squares, Cycle Dublin Bike Tour is a unique and eco-friendly way to see most of Dublin in just two and a half hours. Led by Colin, a qualified Fáilte Ireland National Tour Guide who studied Irish Culture & Heritage, the tour covers most of Dublin's incredible past in great detail. Electric bike tours are available for an additional fee. Tours begin at 10.30am and 2pm, 7-days a week.

ESCAPE ROOM

Escape Dublin

Best for:
Puzzle solvers.
bleat.taxi.wide

Fancy your hand at some witchcraft and wizardry or helping Sherlock solve a complex crime or even racing to find a cure to save the world? Escape Dublin's themed rooms will have you working as a team to solve puzzles and escape the locked room before the 60-minute timer comes to an end and you're left stuck forever (some of that may be exaggerated...). Groups of up to 6 people are allowed with prices ranging from €20 to €29 per person, depending on the number of escapees.

Vintage Tea Trips

GRAFTON STREET, ST STEPHEN'S GREEN & PORTOBELLO

Iveagh Gardens

LIVE MUSIC

Whelan's Live Music Venue 18

Best for:
Discovering new musical artists.
▪ talent.relax.again

Whelan's claim to be Dublin's original live music venue and a big reason for the city becoming a cornerstone of international music. Over its many years showcasing artists from around the world, past performers include Arctic Monkeys and Damien Rice. It was actually at one of Rice's shows, that a young Ed Sheeran had his *'musical epiphany'* to pursue a life in the music industry. Open late 7-nights a week, Whelan's entertains Dubliners and visitors all year round, bringing musicians from all genres to its historic stage.

GARDENS

Iveagh Gardens 19

Best for:
Escaping the city.
▪ resist.hulk.safety

Considered one of Dublin's 'hidden gems', the gardens were designed in 1865 and combine French formal and English landscape styles. A collection of features, including rustic grottos, woodland, a rose garden, a yew maze, and sunken lawns with fountain centrepieces can be seen. The highlight has to be the cascading 'waterfall' water feature, which has 32 rock samples – one from each county in Ireland. Entry into the gardens is free, however events are often held here which may require an admission fee.

PERFORMING ARTS

National Concert Hall 20

Best for:
Eclectic music lovers.
▪ living.ships.space

Since opening in 1981, the hall has established itself as one of the best-rated performing arts venues across Europe. Musicians from all genres are welcomed, from touring orchestras to lively jazz bands to traditional Irish artists. With events on most days and no dress code, visitors can experience world-class performances in a relaxed and welcoming atmosphere. So, whether you're curious about Ireland's long musical heritage, adore classical music or simply love music of all genres, this is the place for you!

CINEMA

The Stella Cinema Rathmines 21

Best for:
Rainy days.
▪ motion.loaded.shrimp

Fit with plush leather armchairs, sofas and even beds, there's nothing like a visit to the Stella Cinema on a lazy, rainy day. Originally opened in the 1920s, the interior has been restored to reflect the glitz and glam of the era but with all the modern amenities you need. With only one screen, this is a far more intimate and cosy experience than the big cinema chains. Open 7-days a week, you can catch everything from new blockbusters to old Hollywood classics here.

GRAFTON STREET, ST STEPHEN'S GREEN & PORTOBELLO

WALKING TOUR
ST STEPHEN'S GREEN

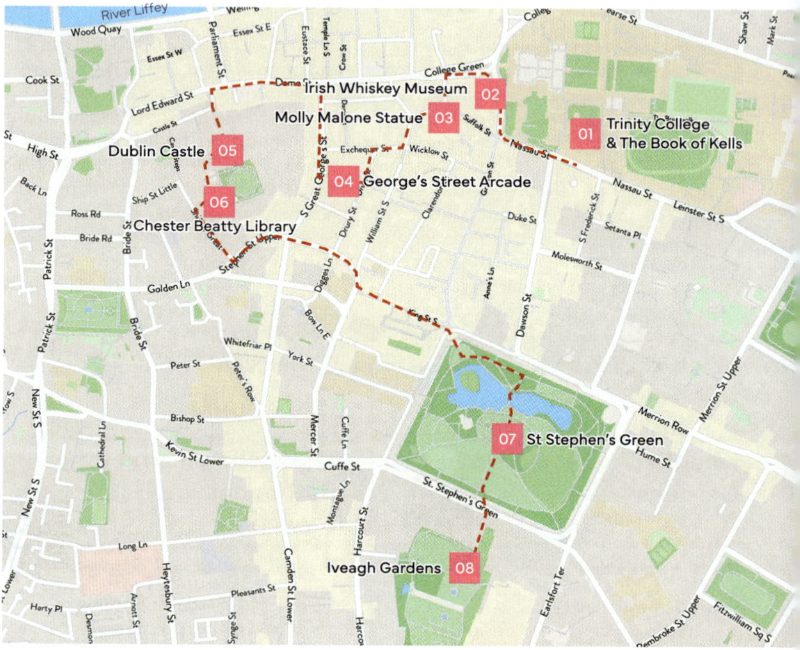

GRAFTON STREET, ST STEPHEN'S GREEN & PORTOBELLO

Starting at College Green and ending in the enchanting Iveagh Gardens, this 3km route showcases Dublin's iconic landmarks. History buffs, architecture lovers, and outdoor enthusiasts will revel in this vibrant city walk. Don't miss giving the Molly Malone statue a cheeky touch for good luck—why not eh? The tranquil St. Stephen's Green Park and picturesque Iveagh Gardens offer a perfect escape from the city buzz.

WALKING TOUR

TOTAL LENGTH: 3KM

DURATION: 40 MINS (NO STOPS)

TERRAIN: FLAT PAVEMENT

STARTING POINT: TRINITY COLLEGE

END POINT: IVEAGH GARDENS

01
TRINITY COLLEGE

06
CHESTER BEATTY LIBRARY

02
IRISH WHISKEY MUSEUM

07
ST STEPHEN'S GREEN PARK

03
MOLLY MALONE STATUE

08
IVEAGH GARDENS

04
GEORGE'S STREET ARCADE

TIME FOR A BREAK?

Worked up an appetite? Take a break at **Mani** located near to George's Street Arcade. You can rest your legs whilst devouring some of Dublin's best pizza!

05
DUBLIN CASTLE

GRAFTON STREET, ST STEPHEN'S GREEN & PORTOBELLO

MEMORABLE MOMENT:
An enjoyable jewellery making experience at Silver Works!

GRAFTON STREET, ST STEPHEN'S GREEN & PORTOBELLO

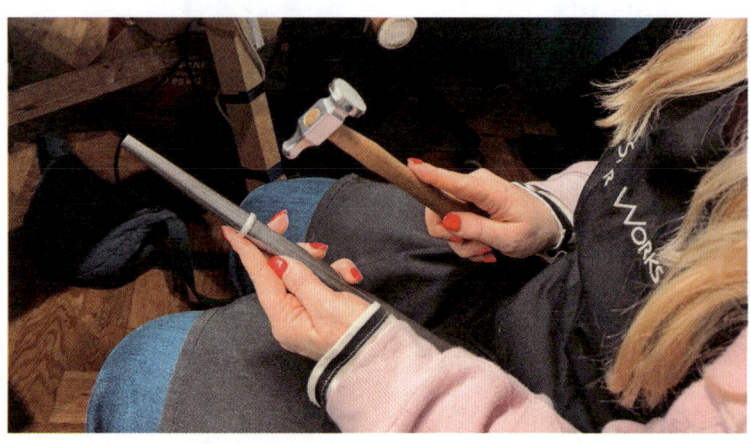

BY NO FUSS TRAVEL EDITOR, LAURA MAYES

Firstly, we filled our faces with pizza across the road at Mani, which we would highly recommend, *(I went with the potato & rosemary, with a hot chilli & honey dip! Don't worry, they also offer the usual margherita and pepperoni options).* We then headed to Silver Works jewellery store on Drury Street to take on the 'forge a silver ring workshop' – a hands-on experience, that promised creativity and craftsmanship. During the two-hour workshop, we began by sawing through a strip of silver to size it correctly. We used a variety of tools and techniques, including sanding, hammering, and filing, to complete our rings. While the professionals made each step look incredibly easy, we found it a bit fiddly at times. Nevertheless, we left with something personal and memorable to hold on to. The workshops vary in length from two hours to a full day and are offered at two locations, both in Dublin. It's an ideal experience for special occasions, such as a hen party, as they also host private group workshops. Overall, it was a lovely and unique experience that we would recommend if you're looking for something a little different.

> **"** Overall, the silver ring workshop was a lovely and unique experience that we would recommend if you're looking for something a little different. **"**

LGBTQIA+ BAR 22

Mother Club at LoSt LaNe

▪ vibrate.breed.terms

Starting back in 2010, Mother has grown into an institution within Dublin's LGBTQIA+ club nights. Now held at LoSt LaNe, the club and its festivals have attracted major artists, including Lily Allen, Scissor Sisters and Anitta. Make sure to pack your dancing shoes, you'll need them here!

BAR & RESTAURANT 23

The Bank on College Green

▪ select.hosts.starts

Once a grand Victorian banking hall, they now welcome guests into its historic hall for great food in an atmosphere like no other – how often can a restaurant claim to have vaults in its basement! Serving breakfast, lunch and dinner every day, there's never a bad time to visit this spot.

IRISH/FRENCH BISTRO 24

Pichet

▪ claims.shack.expose

Pichet offers a modern twist on the classic bistro, blending French and Irish cuisines to create unique dishes. Seasonally changing and using ingredients from local Irish suppliers, the menu offers excellent value for a Michelin Guide dining experience! They're open 7-days a week.

PUB 25

The Stags Head

▪ sleeps.pest.unable

Another traditional Irish pub offering traditional Irish food and music, except this ones award-winning *(awarded Ireland's best traditional pub of the year 2023)*. The Stag's Head dates back to 1780 and has a charming old-world interior, complete with three floors of bars.

LGBTQIA+ BAR 26

The George

▪ notes.castle.gained

The George has been a staple of Dublin's LGBTQIA+ scene for 40+ years thanks to its huge dancefloor, day-time bar and nationally recognised drag acts. With themed events each night of the week, including the legendary Sunday Bingo with 'Shirley Temple Bar', there's never a dull day at The George!

Mani

PIZZA

PI Pizza (George's Street)

■ flags.dare.move

Delicious wood-fired pizza made with local, and artisan produce including buffalo mozzarella from Toons Bridge Dairy, Co. Cork; Achill Island sea salt; and chorizo from Fingal Ferguson's Gubbeen Smokehouse, Co. Cork. As well as pizza's, they offer a small selection of drinks and desserts.

MEDITERRANEAN

Kicky's

■ rent.number.meal

Bright colours and in your face flavours make up the experience at Kicky's. Whitewashed brick walls and bold pop art dominate the interior while the Michelin Guide menu makes for a one-of-a-kind feast. Evening slots book up fast here so make sure to reserve in advance!

CHEESE & WINE

Loose Canon Cheese & Wine

■ tennis.mason.supply

Located next to George's St. Arcade, this small but stylish dining space offer, you guessed it, a wide selection of cheese and wine! Highly rated cheese toasties are also on offer if you're after something a little more substantial. Please note they don't accept bookings here.

PIZZA — EDITORS CHOICE

Mani

■ patch.wizard.drain

From food truck to a favourite in the Grafton Street area, Mani has earned its spot as one of Dublin's best pizza-by-the-slice joints. With its Roman-style dough fermented for three days, every slice is perfectly crisp and packed with flavour. They're open 7-days a week until sell out.

PUB

Grogan's

■ swift.atomic.debit

One of the few pubs in Dublin with no TV or loud music dominating the room, expect great craic with a visit to Grogan's. Famed for its Irish cheddar cheese and ham toastie, it's the perfect place to refuel after a day wandering the city streets. Grogan's is open 7-days a week.

SEAFOOD RESTAURANT

SOLE Seafood & Grill

■ meals.hits.many

SOLE offers a first-rate dining experience in Dublin, serving Ireland's finest seafood and premium meats in a warm, welcoming atmosphere. SOLE's menu includes fresh Irish oysters, lobster and more, all locally sourced and expertly prepared. Please note they have a smart casual dress code.

BAR & RESTAURANT 〖33〗

Bootleg

silver.comical.feeds

Get ready to "drink, dance, dine" as Bootleg's motto proudly suggests, likely in that very order! Taking over a former Starbucks, this independent bar serves up a varied drinks menu, a tapas-inspired spread mixing Mediterranean/Asian flavours and plenty of space to boogie the night away.

BAR & RESTAURANT 〖34〗

Fade Street Social

august.builds.duke

Fade Street Social, led by celebrity chef Dylan McGrath, showcases Irish produce through inventive small plates and hearty dishes. With a gastro bar, wood-fired restaurant, cocktail bar and rooftop terrace, pretty much all your needs are covered here!

PUB — **LOCALS CHOICE** 〖35〗

The Long Hall

many.amused.fields

Standing as one of Dublin's oldest pubs, the Long Hall has built a reputation of being one of the city's very best spots for a drink (no food served here). In fact, Bruce Springsteen claims the pub is his favourite in Dublin and pops by any time he's touring across the pond!

KOREAN 〖36〗

Chimac

pipe.river.basis

Did you know, people in Korea love fried chicken and beer so much that they created a whole word for it – chimac? Well, this spot lives up to half of its name, there's no beers but there are plenty of fried chicken options, as well as burgers and indulgent sides like chimac poutine.

MEDITERRANEAN — **LOCALS CHOICE** 〖37〗

Uno Mas

ranges.flops.maker

Uno Mas serves up Spanish-inspired small plates with seasonal Irish ingredients. Pair your meal with a glass from their standout sherry list for the complete experience. Closed Sundays and Mondays, it's a popular spot, so booking ahead is definitely recommended.

MEXICAN 〖38〗

Masa (Drury Street)

corn.stiff.jams

For fresh tacos and cracking margaritas, Masa is a winner. Their menu stars house-made tacos loaded with fillings like pork belly or fried cauliflower. Affordable, laid-back and packing punches of flavour, it's perfect for a quick bite or capping off a day of Dublin exploration.

The Long Hall

SMALL PLATES & WINE — LOCALS CHOICE 39

Amy Austin
voted.gaps.couch

Amy Austin's allure of 'wine on tap' is what brought the masses to its doors but since opening in 2020, its food has also pulled in the crowds. The tapas-style menu hits all the right notes – meat, fish, veggie and dessert. Plates are quite small however, so don't arrive absolutely starving (or order a lot!).

PIZZA — 40

BAMBINO (Stephen Street)
beans.cloak.pirate

After falling in love with the 'New York pizza slice' during their visits to the Big Apple as children, the owners of Bambino wanted to bring that flavour to Dublin. It's so good you'll likely face a queue, but trust us, you won't regret it after your first bite! Purchase by the slice or a full 20" pizza!

RESTAURANT — 41

WILDE Restaurant
gangs.limbs.full

WILDE Restaurant serves up the best of Irish produce in a glamorous, green space reminiscent of a 1930s vintage eatery. Named after one of Ireland's most famous playwrights, Oscar Wilde, it's a great option for non-meat eaters, with a dedicated vegan and vegetarian menu.

BAMBINO

PUB — LOCALS CHOICE 42

Neary's Bar & Lounge
deputy.lunch.export

Opened in 1887, with many original features still in place, Neary's is a picture-perfect representation of a quintessential Irish pub. A favourite watering hole among local theatre actors, it's the ideal spot to enjoy a pint, a hearty meal and listen to tales from some of Dublin's finest storytellers.

PUB — 43

Kehoes Pub
goats.mason.skips

Kehoes describes themselves as "A country pub in the heart of the city" and we would say they've nailed that. Despite being steps away from some of Dublin's biggest attractions, once you step inside, you'll feel like you've been whisked away to a quieter, bygone era.

Café | LOCALS CHOICE | 44

Café en Seine

dads.jump.canny

Café en Seine does it all – by day, it's a chilled spot for coffee and lunch; by night, it transforms into one of Dublin's most stylish cocktail bars. With its creative drinks, varied food menu and Gatsby-esque interiors, it's a go-to for any occasion! They're open 7-days a week, but hours vary.

LOCALS CHOICE

Upmarket but affordable **Café en Seine** is a local favourite, with simple burger, soup and sandwich style lunches and technicoloured cocktails in a palatial environment. The whole thing feels a lot like getting champagne on a lager budget.

LOCAL WRITER, JAMES HENDICOTT

STEAKHOUSE | 45

Featherblade Steakhouse

upgrading.shaky.beans

All about quality cuts cooked to perfection, Featherblade Steakhouse serves some of the best steaks and burgers in Dublin at surprisingly reasonable prices. It's not just the mains that shine here either, the sides are spot on – with the truffle mac and cheese stealing the show!

HEALTHY BOWLS | 46

Sprout & Co (Dawson Street)

jazz.rests.props

"Eating well should never sacrifice taste. Truly good food is properly delicious too" – this is the rallying cry behind Sprout & Co. Sourcing produce from its own organic farm in Kildare, eating here is proof that healthy doesn't mean boring – it's real food, done properly.

FINE DINING | 47

Library Street Restaurant

swear.hoot.loaf

"Everything is meant to be shared" is the mantra of Library Street Restaurant. The regularly changing menu proudly includes local ingredients crafted into French, Irish and Italian courses. As a Michelin Guide eatery, your best bet is to book well in advance to bag yourself a seat here!

CAFÉ | 48

Beanhive (Dawson Street)

jump.gates.best

Beanhive is home to hearty breakfasts, sweet snacks, huge sandwiches and plenty of speciality coffees for those looking for their caffeine fix. All prepared with local, fresh ingredients, everyone is welcome here with great vegan and gluten free options available!

MIDDLE EASTERN `EDITORS CHOICE` 🌿 49

Tang (Dawson Street)

▪ bake.dash.track

With its commitment to serving up delicious dishes whilst focusing on sustainability, Tang brings a feel-good approach that is matched by its tasty, varied flavours. Whether you're in the mood for pancakes, shawarma or a build-your-own salad, get yourself down to Tang!

FINE DINING 🌿 50

Glovers Alley

▪ fight.poems.sprint

Found in the beautiful Fitzwilliam Hotel, overlooking St Stephen's Green, Glovers Alley has a modern yet old-fashioned, 1930s-like swagger to it. With a Michelin star to its name, this is fine dining at its best – led by world-class chef Andy McFadden and his expert team.

CHINESE/TAIWANESE 51

BIGFAN

▪ places.pound.rivers

BIGFAN blends Chinese and Taiwanese flavours with a bright, colourful interior for a fun meal out. Whether the wagyu cheeseburger or the vegan Jiaozi have you salivating, the extensive Michelin Guide menu will please even the pickiest of eaters! We recommend booking ahead.

TAPAS `LOCALS CHOICE` 52

Bar Pez

▪ crisis.vest.filed

When stepping through the door of Bar Pez, it really feels like you've been whisked away to a quaint local restaurant in a rural Spanish village. Small plates focusing on seafood reign supreme here while the extensive wine list offers a suitable way to wash it all down! Closed on Tuesdays.

SUSHI 53

Zakura Noodle & Sushi

▪ party.games.supply

Enjoy fresh sushi, ramen, and Japanese delights at Zakura Noodle & Sushi. Great for a quick bite or a proper sit-down meal, guests can bring their own drinks with a small corkage fee – perfect for some cosy dining in this small, intimate spot! They're open 7-days a week.

SPANISH 54

La Gordita

▪ serve.types.during

Authentic Spanish cooking in a Bodega-style setting is what awaits guests of La Gordita. Perfect for both a relaxed meal or a special occasion, La Gordita combines simple, delicious dishes with a carefully chosen wine list for a well-rounded dining experience.

Tang

RESTAURANT & ROOFTOP BAR 55

Sophie's Dublin

issues.nobody.activism

Looking for breathtaking views from brunch till late? Sophie's, found atop the Dean Hotel, offers 360° views of Dublin in its stylish restaurant and bar. Choose from a wide-ranging menu for food and drink the night away with their extensive cocktail, wine, beer and soft drinks selection.

PUB 56

Devitt's

prop.limbs.rails

Looking to hear some proper Irish music? Head to Devitt's. The traditional Irish pub showcases some of the best local artists every day of the week. Combine that with the delicious Irish comfort food and the best pint of Guinness in Dublin (their claim!) and you've got yourself the perfect evening.

ASIAN 57

Neon Asian Street Food

aura.moving.humans

Neon Asian Street Food started back in 2012 with the goal of offering good quality food at good prices. Taking inspiration from Thailand, Singapore, Vietnam and more, a visit here is like taking a mini food tour of Southeast Asia. Oh, you'll also get a free ice cream cone with every order – result!

CHINESE 58

Hang Dai Chinese

twig.barn.speeds

Hang Dai Chinese delivers a blend of Chinese-inspired dishes with a contemporary twist, perfect for sharing with friends, family or partners. As the night goes on, the restaurant transitions into a party atmosphere with DJs taking to the decks, so wear your dancing shoes!

BRUNCH 59

Ebb&Flow Camden

◨ mess.chained.mess

Ebb & Flow Camden is loved for its barista-quality coffee, fluffy pancakes and relaxed vibe. With friendly service and a cosy atmosphere, it's a brilliant spot to enjoy a casual brunch or a quick caffeine fix. Tables are available on a walk-ins only basis, bookings are not accepted.

HEALTHY BOWLS   60

Sprout & Co (Camden Street)

◨ outer.lace.shapes

"Eating well should never sacrifice taste. Truly good food is properly delicious too" – this is the rallying cry behind Sprout & Co. Sourcing produce from its own organic farm in Kildare, eating here is proof that healthy doesn't mean boring – it's real food, done properly.

BARBECUE & GRILL 61

Mister S

◨ gaps.hooked.pets

Literally bringing the heat, Mister S serves up wood-fired and charcoal-grilled dishes with a 2-course minimum order. Titled 'Meal of the Year' by the Irish Independent, here you can indulge in some of the best meat in Dublin, as well as their signature burnt end rendang spring rolls.

Sprout & Co

CHICKEN 62

Camden Rotisserie

◨ chimp.facing.doctor

A family-owned and run chicken shop, Camden Rotisserie has been delivering top-class chicken dishes to Dubliners for over a decade. Far more than just 'fried chicken and chips', patrons can dine out on everything from juicy wraps to fresh salads to towering burgers.

ITALIAN 63

Sprezzatura

◨ pans.bound.asks

Sprezzatura mixes Italian ideas with Irish produce to create some of the freshest and tastiest pasta in all of Dublin. The menu, which regularly changes, typically features gnocchi, arancini and a wide range of pasta dishes, all perfect for refuelling after a long day on your feet!

IRISH RESTAURANT · LOCALS CHOICE · 64

Delahunt

moons.same.spoil

From its humble beginnings as a grocer's shop, which was mentioned in James Joyce's Ulysses, Delahunt has come a long way. Today it is a Michelin Guide eatery that offers its guests a limited but indulgent menu – from wild venison to crispy ox tongue, it's a great choice for adventurous eaters!

INDIAN · LOCALS CHOICE · 65

Pickle

advice.minds.with

Inspired by the tastes of Northern India, Pickle is led by Chef Sunil Ghai and promises its guests flavours and textures out of this world. Combine the fantastic food with its attentive staff, and there's no wonder why it features as one of Dublin's Michelin Guide restaurants!

LEBANESE · 66

Damascus Gate

short.scope.tiger

Damascus Gate brings the flavours of the Middle East to the streets of Dublin. From mains of aromatic stews and kebabs to falafel and halloumi sides, you're sure to leave this eatery with a happy stomach and a smile on your face. They're open 7-days a week from 12pm-11pm.

BAKERY & Café · 67

The Bretzel Bakery & Café

ample.duck.metals

Established in 1870, The Bretzel Bakery & Café is a staple of Dublin and the place to go to get your bread, pastry or cake fix. Open 7-days a week, here you can grab the freshest, fluffiest sandwiches and delicious cakes in a cosy café environment. Their sourdough bread is top tier!

MICHELIN STAR · LOCALS CHOICE · 68

Bastible Restaurant

newest.each.chip

Bastible prides itself on its relaxed decor that allows its food to take centre stage. With a Michelin star under its belt and almost ten years of service, Bastible continues to set the benchmark of modern dining in Dublin. Availability is limited so it's best to make a reservation.

BOARD GAME BAR & CAFÉ · 69

Board Dublin

speeds.lace.dates

A dream destination for board game buffs, Board Dublin is exactly what its name suggests – a lively games bar and café. With over 200 games to choose from, even the pickiest players are sure to find a favourite! *P.S if you're a board game lover, why not buy our very own 'Road Trip: The Game'.*

167

Wren Urban Nest

POD HOTEL 70

Wren Urban Nest

+353 1 223 4555

forms.empty.agrees

Ireland's first net carbon-neutral hotel! This eco-friendly haven might have pocket-sized rooms, but they're chic and stylish none the less, thanks to the Scandinavian-inspired décor. Head to the on-site ALT restaurant for delicious brunch options.

HOTEL 71

Maldron Hotel Kevin Street

+353 1 906 8900

pits.avoid.spice

Located right across the street from St. Patrick's Cathedral, Maldron Hotel Kevin Street provides stylish, modern rooms in a prime city spot. Make sure to take advantage of the hearty breakfasts served every morning to fuel your day of Dublin exploration!

HOTEL 72

Radisson Blu Royal Hotel, Dublin

+353 1 898 2900

front.scare.moral

If relaxation and rejuvenation top your to-do list for your Dublin trip, the 4-star Radisson Blu Royal Hotel is the perfect choice. Here, guests can enjoy a bar, grill, lounge and even a spa area – all without stepping foot outside!

HOTEL & APARTMENTS 73

Drury Court Hotel

+353 1 475 1988

posts.dads.nights

One of the few family-run hotels still remaining in Dublin, Drury Court Hotel is a charming 3-star boutique hotel. Both rooms and whole apartments are available here, making it a great spot for families or groups travelling together.

HOTEL

The Grafton Hotel

+353 1 255 2700

■ yarn.card.photo

The Grafton Hotel is a modern, art-deco-style accommodation with 128 luxurious rooms in the heart of Dublin. Features include a bar and restaurant, contactless check-in and easy access to many of the city's main attractions.

HOTEL

Marlin Hotel St Stephen's Green

+353 1 522 2000

■ salt.skirt.brand

With the tagline 'Don't just stay… Live,' Marlin Hotel St Stephen's Green offers more than a place to sleep – featuring a lively restaurant (private dining available), a unique coffee horsebox and a dedicated co-working space for its guests.

HOTEL

Stauntons on the Green

+353 1 478 2300

■ react.hunter.points

Housed across 3 refurbished Georgian townhouses overlooking both St Stephen's Green and Iveagh Gardens, this hotel is a calming oasis in the centre of Dublin. With large rooms decorated in Georgian style, you'll feel like royalty during your stay here.

HOTEL

The Green Hotel

+353 1 607 3600

■ rests.magma.post

Freshly refurbished, the Green Hotel is one of Dublin's premier 4-star boutique hotels found a few steps from St Stephen's Green. From comfy, luxury rooms to a 24/7 gym to an on-site chic cocktail bar, you're fully covered with a stay here!

HOTEL

Iveagh Garden Hotel

+353 1 568 5500

■ mice.sleep.stays

The Iveagh Garden Hotel prides itself on offering a 'modern take on traditional luxury' and can be found just off Grafton Street. With over 145 luxurious rooms to choose from and plenty of food and drink options, you may never want to leave!

HOTEL

Clayton Hotel Charlemont

+353 1 960 6700

■ deeper.valley.prove

Clayton Hotel Charlemont offers a stylish, riverside retreat with modern rooms, a decent fitness centre and an on-site restaurant and bar. Ideally located, it's away from crowds but still within walking distance of Dublin's top attractions.

Merrion Square & Fitzwilliam Square

Looking to indulge? The Merrion Square & Fitzwilliam Square area promises a blend of sophistication and charm. Enjoy a leisurely stroll through the squares, savour exquisite dishes at top-tier restaurants and stay in luxury accommodation.

MERRION SQUARE & FITZWILLIAM SQUARE:
Cultural attractions, luxury & fine dining.

Considered to be one of Dublin's more upscale districts, Merrion Square & Fitzwilliam Square is the place to stay if you fancy a 'treat yourself' kind of city break. Some of the city's best cultural attractions can be found here, from the National Gallery of Ireland to the National Concert Hall to Royal Hibernian Academy of Arts. Enjoy a stay at the many 4-and-5-star hotels like the Merrion Hotel Dublin (complete with a spa!) or the eccentric but very welcoming Number 31. And for food? Well, when it comes to fine dining, you're spoilt for choice. Enjoy some of the finest French cuisine this side of the channel at Dax Restaurant or award-winning seafood from the beloved Matt The Thresher.

TOP 5 THINGS TO SEE & DO

01
THE LITTLE MUSEUM OF DUBLIN

02
NATIONAL GALLERY OF IRELAND

03
SWENY'S PHARMACY

04
MERRION SQUARE PARK

05
OSCAR WILDE HOUSE

GETTING HERE

Approx. Walking Distance From: Merrion Square
O'Connell St (20 mins), Smithfield (38 mins), The Liberties (37 mins), Temple Bar (23 mins), St Stephen's Green (14 mins), Grand Canal Dock (16 mins)

Dart & Commuter Trains
Stop: Pearse Station (10 min walk)

Bus Routes to Merrion Square: 120, 145, 15A, 15B, 26
Stops: Merrion Square South, Merrion Square, Merrion Square North, Holles Street, Baggot Street Lower, Fitzwilliam Street, Merrion Square West

MERRION SQUARE & FITZWILLIAM SQUARE

HISTORICAL VENUE

Sweny's Pharmacy

Best for:
Lovers of literary.

glitz.moved.sport

A literary landmark frozen in time, Sweny's has transformed from a place of medicine to one that celebrates Dublin's scholarly past. The pharmacy was made famous in James Joyce's 1922 novel Ulysses and now showcases his and other author's iconic works. Maintaining its original Victorian style, today it is run by volunteers who often wear white chemist coats and read aloud passages of Joyce's words. If you're lucky enough, you might even get to hear a traditional Irish ditty from the shop's owner!

ART GALLERY

National Gallery of Ireland

Best for:
Art lovers.

sofa.rider.senior

A must-visit for anyone with even a passing interest in art, the National Gallery of Ireland is home to over 16,000 works, with pieces from Monet, Caravaggio and iconic Irish artists like Jack B. Yeats. Found just off Merrion Square and free to enter every day of the week, it's the ideal place to find some peace and quiet or escape a rainy Dublin day. Here you'll find a range of permanent collections, ever-changing temporary exhibitions, workshops, free guided tours and a cosy café!

LIBRARY

National Library of Ireland

Best for:
Book worms.

cones.drip.bucket

Stunning inside and out, the National Library of Ireland is an absolute must-visit for any lovers of the written word and architecture enthusiasts. Established in 1877, the library collects and preserves Irish literature as well as putting on changing exhibitions and workshops. The iconic reading rooms are open to the public too, just make sure to register for a free Reader's Ticket in advance. You won't be able to borrow any books but its interior, collections of Irish literature and educational exhibitions make it well worth popping by on your trip!

LOCALS CHOICE

"A pharmacy frozen in time that hosts regular readings, **Sweny's Chemist** is maintained as it was in the 1850s in tribute to its role in James Joyce's inaccessible Ulysses, glass bottles, lemon soap and all."

LOCAL WRITER, JAMES HENDICOTT

MUSEUM

National Museum of Ireland - Archaeology 4

Best for:
Celtic history lessons.

ants.tubes.chimp

Journey back to 7,000 BC during your visit to Dublin's Archaeology branch of the National Museum of Ireland. Opened in 1890, the museum will take you through Ireland's long history via its extensive archaeological collections. From St Patrick's Bell, Tara Brooch and 'bog bodies' from 2,000 BC, you'll discover a side of Ireland like you've never seen before. It's free to enter and open 7-days a week. For any self-confessed 'history nerds,' this is a spot you'll want to pop by at least once during your trip!

MUSEUM

National Museum of Ireland - Natural History 5

Best for:
Animal & history fans.

hours.broken.volume

You'd be forgiven if you thought that getting up close and personal with wolves, snakes and other wild creatures would be out of reach during a trip to Dublin. Well, we have some good news – if you like that kind of stuff! The National Museum of Ireland - Natural History is home to a collection of around two million scientific specimens. Affectionately (questionably so) named the 'Dead Zoo', the museum first opened its doors to the public in 1857 and has been wowing and educating its visitors ever since!

National Museum of Ireland - Archaeology

PUBLIC PARK

Merrion Square Park 6

Best for:
Quiet walks.

drove.libraries.today

Escape the city buzz with a visit to Merrion Square, a beautiful Georgian park surrounded by old townhouses. Within the park, visitors can take in its scenic flowers, follow its easy-to-navigate paths and even keep a lookout for a reclining Oscar Wilde statue! If you can, try and pop by on a Sunday when local artists sell their best works outside the park. Running all year round from 10am to 5pm each Sunday, the Merrion Square Open Air Art Gallery is a great way to get to know and support local artists.

175

MERRION SQUARE & FITZWILLIAM SQUARE

TOUR

Oscar Wilde House (7)

Best for:
Stepping back in time.

crew.saints.whips

Across the road from the Oscar Wilde statue within Merrion Square Park, sits Oscar Wilde's childhood home, where you'll find the poet and playwright's top floor nursery. Today the building houses the American College Dublin, however, they are open for public visits on Saturdays and Sundays ONLY, where you'll be able to explore all four floors of history. Tickets are available upon arrival at reception; however, if you'd prefer, you can book ahead online. Concession tickets are available.

Oscar Wilde Statue

ART GALLERY

Royal Hibernian Academy of Arts (8)

Best for:
Rainy days.

blues.paused.grab

Founded over 200 years ago by Irish artists, the Royal Hibernian Academy of Arts has built a legacy of showcasing the very best of Irish and international art, from famous creators to unknown artists. With five galleries, there's a little something for all art lovers – from the Ashford Gallery where new Dublin artists are introduced to the changing exhibits from international superstars. Closed on Mondays, entry is always free, with a deli and wine bar on site to refuel at after your visit!

MUSEUM   EDITORS CHOICE

The Little Museum of Dublin (9)

Best for: An entertaining education of Irish history.

settle.danger.cheek

Over a period of 29 minutes (yep, to be exact), visitors of the Little Museum of Dublin are treated to a rendition of Irish history like no other. The famous guided tours are a celebration of great Irish storytelling, where you'll hear tales from Queen Victoria's visit to Dublin, the rise of U2 and you might even bump into James Joyce and John F. Kennedy! The tours run 7-days a week but as this museum is so popular, you'll definitely need to book in advance. They also host special events.

The Little Museum of Dublin

NIGHTLIFE VENUE

The Sugar Club

Best for: Live music, DJ's & movie screenings.

🟩 tender.trails.clots

(11)

A Dublin musical institution known for its intimate atmosphere, excellent sound, and plush interior, The Sugar Club specialises in genres such as jazz, soul, hip-hop, and world music. Over the last 20 years, the venue has cemented its place as one of Dublin's premier nightlife destinations, hosting artists such as Hozier, The Script, and Roy Ayers. From movie screenings to live DJs on the outdoor terrace, The Sugar Club boasts an exciting & eclectic events calendar. Check and book tickets in advance.

GEORGIAN SQUARE

Fitzwilliam Square

(10)

**Best for:
A city stroll.**

🟩 formed.values.master

Once the largest of Dublin's great Georgian squares, Fitzwilliam Square was built in the early 19th century by William Dargan, the founder of the National Gallery and artist Jack B. Yeats. Sadly, the park is only open to local residents, some of whom pay almost €1,000 a year for the privilege! Some public events do take place in the park so keep an eye out for those. Otherwise, architecture enthusiasts will enjoy taking in the Georgian homes surrounding the park. Don't miss a photo of 46 Fitzwilliam Square!

MUSEUM

National Print Museum

(12)

**Best for:
A one-of-a-kind museum visit.**

🟩 swaps.slam.splice

The museum aims to 'champion print and its impact on the world', with its collection, which is largely made up of letterpress printing equipment. Visitors on guided tours are invited to pull their own letterpress keepsake (for a small fee). Those just wanting to take a look around can enter for free. The creative amongst us might appreciate a visit here (or just those looking to dodge the rain), followed by a visit to the Press Café for some homemade treats. They're closed on Mondays and bank holiday weekends.

MERRION SQUARE & FITZWILLIAM SQUARE

WALKING TOUR

MERRION SQUARE & FITZWILLIAM SQUARE

Embark on a delightful stroll through two of Dublin's most extraordinary squares! This light and leisurely walk takes you past stunning Georgian architecture, immerses you in captivating history, and unveils the charm of the city's former upper-class residential quarters. Along the way, you'll see the magnificent Leinster House and the Department of the Taoiseach – both pivotal to Ireland's parliamentary heritage.

WALKING TOUR

TOTAL LENGTH: 1.4KM

DURATION: 25 MINS (NO STOPS)

TERRAIN: FLAT PAVEMENT

STARTING POINT: MUSEUM OF ARCHAEOLOGY

END POINT: FITZWILLIAM SQUARE

MERRION SQUARE & FITZWILLIAM SQUARE

01
NATIONAL MUSEUM OF IRELAND - ARCHAEOLOGY

06
NATIONAL MUSEUM - NATURAL HISTORY

02
NATIONAL LIBRARY OF IRELAND

07
LITTLE MUSEUM OF DUBLIN

03
SWENY'S PHARMACY

08
FITZWILLIAM SQUARE

04
OSCAR WILDE HOUSE

05
MERRION SQUARE PARK

TIME FOR A BREAK?

Worked up a thirst? Take a break at **Kennedy's Bar & Pub** located opposite Sweny's Pharmacy! Put your feet up and enjoy a pint before you continue your walk.

179

MEMORABLE MOMENT:
Admiring Dublin's Georgian grandeur

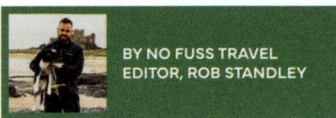

BY NO FUSS TRAVEL EDITOR, ROB STANDLEY

The first couple of times I explored Dublin, I overlooked the beauty and grandeur of Merrion Square and Fitzwilliam Square. As a much younger *(and definitely more handsome)* traveller, I was more interested in Dublin's nightlife than its architecture, museums, and history. Fast forward the best part of a decade, and I returned to Dublin knowing I had to get out on foot to truly appreciate this magnificent area of the city.

My partner Jasmin and I set off on our very own walking tour. Like most of Dublin, this leafy neighbourhood is compact and easy to explore on foot. We began at the National Museum of Ireland before heading to its neighbour, the National Library of Ireland. The scale of the buildings here is remarkable. Turning the corner towards Merrion Square, we made a food stop at Mama's Revenge, where we were served two mammoth burritos. After stuffing our faces, we made a slight detour to check out the infamous Sweny's Pharmacy located opposite Kennedy's Pub. Once we'd snapped a couple of photos, we moved on to the wonderful Merrion Square and its...

> **❝** *I returned to Dublin knowing I had to get out on foot to truly appreciate this magnificent area of the city!* **❞**

charming Georgian townhouses. The park offers a peaceful retreat and is home to the Oscar Wilde Memorial, by which we were both bemused. Funnily enough, there was a group of adults in the playpark pushing a man so fast on the swings that he almost completed a full 360-degree loop. After continuing past the impressive Taoiseach's residence and the Little Museum of Dublin *(a very worthwhile experience)*, we ended our walking tour at the equally grand Fitzwilliam Square. Number 46 Fitzwilliam Square is said to be the most photographed door in Ireland! Overall, a rewarding adventure admiring Dublin's grandeur.

MERRION SQUARE & FITZWILLIAM SQUARE | WHERE TO EAT & DRINK

ITALIAN

Ristorante Di Napoli

detect.jolly.mile

Built on the philosophy of using the best ingredients prepared in the simplest way, the dishes at Ristorante Di Napoli bring a taste of Italy to the streets of Dublin. From stone baked pizzas to decadent pasta to healthy salads, this restaurant will please all palates!

PUB & RESTAURANT

Kennedy's Pub & Restaurant

became.hopes.launch

Established in 1850, Kennedy's Pub & Restaurant is steeped in Dublin history, with past patrons including both James Joyce and Samuel Beckett. Here you can expect good ol' pub food, such as fish and chips, burgers and to top it all off, warm apple crumble.

TEX-MEX

Mama's Revenge

moons.stem.amused

Burritos, quesadillas, nachos, tacos and chilli sound like your kind of thing? Then head to Mama's Revenge. We'd recommend if you're looking a filling lunch or early dinner, as we enjoyed some mammoth sized build-your-own burritos! They're closed on Sundays.

BAKERY & PATISSERIE

Hansel and Gretel Bakery & Patisserie

office.stroke.voice

Take-away coffee and bakes to die for! This small but sweet artisan bakery offers up everything from fresh croissants and breads to French style pastries and tarts. The perfect 'grab and go' bite to keep you going as you explore this area. Please note they're closed on Sunday's.

TAPAS

Table 45

friend.successes.asking

Warmly welcoming dogs and their humans, the South American inspired tapas eatery offers tasty, flavour-packed dishes perfect for sharing. Its laid-back atmosphere and extensive menu make it an ideal spot to refuel, whether you're popping in for brunch, dinner or a relaxed drink.

Mama's Revenge

182

FINE DINING

Pearl Brasserie

 bikes.fast.artist

Award-winning fine dining at its best, Pearl Brasserie combines the very best of Irish and French produce to create dishes out of this world. Tucked in a cosy basement on Merrion Street, the atmosphere matches the restaurant's food – classy but still friendly and approachable.

MODERN DINING **LOCALS CHOICE**

Etto

thanks.item.heap

Etto is a Michelin Guide, cosy, rustic restaurant serving up modern dishes with eye catching presentation. Foodies will love this spot, with both a standard menu and a weekly changing chef's menu to pick from. They're open for dinner Monday to Saturday and lunch Thursday to Saturday.

IRISH RESTAURANT

Hugo's

held.lowest.chart

A snug, stylish restaurant perfect for a date night, Hugo's serves up Irish dishes with a modern twist. Using locally sourced, organic ingredients each meal is prepared with the utmost care, while the interior decor will have you feeling like you're in a luxurious 1920s dining club.

Kennedy's Pub & Restaurant

WINE BAR & CAFÉ **LOCALS CHOICE**

Margadh

claps.device.empire

Café by day, wine bar by night. A great spot to unwind after exploring the Royal Hibernian Academy of Arts (RHA) - it's located inside! Enjoy breakfast or lunch on weekdays, except Monday. If wine and small bites are more your speed, swing by from Wednesday to Saturday for a sophisticated meal out in an art gallery!

CASUAL FINE DINING

BANG Restaurant & Wine Bar Dublin

■ stick.rope.strain

Whether you're after a romantic date night spot, a celebratory meal or just a place to fuel up after a day of adventuring in Dublin, BANG has you covered. Priding itself on a 'casual yet elegant' dining style, the menus cover everything from fresh seafood to traditional Irish roasts – dig in!

STEAKHOUSE

Brookwood Steakhouse

■ humble.buyers.error

Offering the highest quality, 100% Irish beef, this one is a must visit for steak lovers! Not your thing? Brookwood also offer a selection of seafood, including Irish oysters, and an extensive wine and cocktail menu, as well as an option for vegetarians. They're open 7-days a week.

ITALIAN

Cirillo's

■ admits.shark.spice

Cirillo's follows the philosophy of keeping its menu short and simple but cooking everything to absolute perfection. Using a pizza oven imported from Naples, you can rest assured that you're getting the real Italian experience here. If pizza isn't your thing, go for the homemade pasta.

COFFEE SHOP

Bear Market Coffee (Pembroke Street)

■ puff.colleague.proof

The ideal coffee stop, Bear Market Coffee is a stylish coffee bar offering the perfect cup of the good stuff, hand roasted in their very own in-house, in-church, coffee roastery. They, in fact, now have 7 coffee bars across Dublin – just bear in mind this one is only open on weekdays.

SEAFOOD

Matt The Thresher

■ late.basic.kick

An award-winning family-owned restaurant serving up a range of dishes and specialising in seafood. Using fresh, locally sourced ingredients, both the food and service here is top-notch. If you're nearby on the weekend, be sure to stop by between 2pm and 5pm to enjoy live jazz music!

PUB

O'Connor's of Mount Street

■ bike.claims.bleat

"Enter a stranger, leave a friend" is the motto of O'Connor's of Mount Street. The traditional Irish pub has everything you want from a cosy watering hole: good people, good food and a warming fireplace! They host a pub quiz every Thursday and live music on a Friday and Saturday evening.

PUB 28

Toners Pub

poet.image.brain

Established in 1818, Toners has no end of Dublin's history weaved into its walls. Legend has it that both literary giants W.B. Yeats and Patrick Kavanagh were regulars. You won't find any food here but according to Rory Guinness, a member of the Guinness family, Toners serve "the best pint of Guinness in Dublin".

SOUTHEAST ASIAN 29

Chai Yo

fairly.sock.shaky

Get a front row seat and watch expert chefs whip up your dishes. Using teppanyaki tables, your food is prepped and cooked (with plenty of fire!) right in front of you. If you're after more of a low-key experience, you can book a table in their dining room and enjoy food from across Southeast Asia!

JAPANESE 30

Zakura Japanese Tapas

heavy.valley.dozen

If you're craving Asian cuisine during your trip to Dublin, Zakura on Baggot Street Lower is a top choice. Known for generous portions and beautifully presented dishes, Zakura's menu covers a range of flavours from rich ramen to fresh sushi and hearty rice bowls.

UNIQUE RESTAURANT 31

Canal Boat Restaurant

owners.shirts.spoken

Set sail on the Grand Canal and enjoy a three-course meal as you pass through historic 225-year-old locks and bridges. Departing at 8pm from Mespil Road, the Canal Boat Restaurant is the perfect way to enjoy good food while taking in one of Dublin's great waterways.

BAR & RESTAURANT 32

Suesey Street

healers.keep.herds

Another great spot for all occasions, Suesey Street is renowned for its Irish cuisine with a European twist. Here you can enjoy excellent food in a classy atmosphere without the formal vibe that can come with some upscale restaurants! Note they are closed on Sunday's.

FINE DINING 33

Dax Restaurant

rush.globe.alone

Featured as a Michelin Guide restaurant, you can be sure of great tastes, pristine presentation and the highest quality ingredients when dining here. The French eatery is found in a cellar of an old townhouse with the interior giving off a classic fine-dining feel to it – bon appétit!

HOTEL 34

The Alex Hotel

+353 1 607 3700

pipes.could.sudden

Mix business with pleasure during a stay at the luxurious Alex Hotel. Its fantastic co-working area with ultra-fast WiFi makes it perfect for those looking to extend their trip while working. There's a range of on-site dining options and room service is available.

HOTEL 35

The Davenport Hotel

+353 1 607 3500

transit.hooks.shift

Blending heritage and history with modern luxury, the Davenport Hotel has it all. From premium dining options, a bar lounge, a 24/7 gym and spacious, elegant bedrooms, a stay here is sure to leave you refreshed and ready to take on Dublin!

HOTEL 36

The Mont Hotel

+353 1 6073800

ranged.logic.update

The Mont combines a chic style with comfort and convenience. With Dublin's top landmarks just steps away, you're perfectly positioned to explore here. Don't forget to enjoy a tipple at the on-site Sin Bin Bar or make the most of the 24/7 gym, too!

HOTEL 37

The Leinster

+353 1 233 6000

hills.soap.pine

Chic, bold bedrooms and swanky suites await guests of the Leinster, found just off Merrion Square. Expect warm welcomes throughout this modern hotel. Treat yourself to one of the dining packages during your stay for a real culinary treat!

HOTEL 38

The Draper Rooms

+353 86 813 9588

discrepancy.poetic.rocket

The Draper Rooms is a family-run boutique hotel above the cosy O'Connors of Mount Street pub. Expect a warm Irish welcome from staff and locals – though keep in mind evenings can be lively when the pub gets busy!

HOTEL 39

The Merrion Hotel Dublin

+353 1 603 0600

milky.cost.bound

Created from combining four Georgian townhouses, the Merrion Hotel Dublin is a sanctuary of luxury. The 5-star hotel offers beautiful bedrooms, a spa and health club and even an on-site 2-star Michelin restaurant!

HOTEL 40

Conrad Dublin

+353 1 602 8900

ground.fans.bliss

Overlooking the iconic National Concert Hall, Conrad Dublin is a luxury 5-star hotel that offers spacious rooms and suites (the largest in Dublin), 3 restaurants and a fitness centre. Oh, and pups are welcome too (2 dogs per room)!

HOTEL 41

Number 31

+353 1 676 5011

long.loft.down

Eccentric with oodles of personality, Number 31 mixes luxurious Georgian style with a minimalist twist. Once said to be home to one of Dublin's best party scenes in the swinging 60s, today guests can enjoy comfy rooms, fresh breakfast and a beautiful garden.

BED & BREAKFAST 42

Kilronan House

+353 1 475 5266

expert.strut.spun

Built in 1834, Kilronan House is a time capsule of upper class Dublin during the Georgian age. Inside, guests will find original decor, plush rooms and an award-winning breakfast served up each morning. Book direct for the best rates.

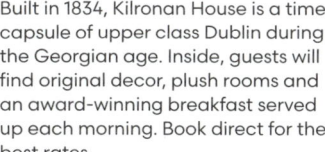

The Merrion Hotel

The Docklands

With a mix of old industrial charm and sleek modern architecture, the Docklands offer a more relaxed atmosphere, making it a perfect spot to unwind after a day of sightseeing. Don't worry, you'll still be close enough to the action and nearby attractions.

PAGES 188 - 207

THE DOCKLANDS:
Dublin's vibrant yet relaxed waterfront district.

If you're looking for a lively blend of modern attractions and a glimpse into Ireland's rich history, Dublin's Docklands is the perfect spot. Once the bustling centre of the city's shipping and industrial scene, this vibrant area is now packed with exciting experiences. Explore the EPIC The Irish Emigration Museum, where the powerful stories of Ireland's emigrants are brought to life, or head to the historic Jeanie Johnston to learn about the city's famine past. For those feeling adventurous, hop aboard a boat tour or try your hand at some watersports along the River Liffey. If you're after a bit of peace and quiet, take a relaxing stroll along the Great South Wall to Poolbeg Lighthouse, where you'll be rewarded with stunning panoramic views. Whether you're enjoying a craft beer at one of the many riverside bars, reflecting at the Famine Memorial, or simply soaking in the atmosphere, the Docklands is an essential stop on any Dublin visit. Don't miss out on all the action in this unique and evolving area!

TOP 5 THINGS TO SEE & DO

01
URBAN BREWING TOURS

02
EPIC THE IRISH EMIGRATION MUSEUM

03
THE JEANIE JOHNSTON

04
GRAND CANAL DOCK

05
POOLBEG LIGHTHOUSE

GETTING HERE

Approx. Walking Distance From: Grand Canal Dock
O'Connell St (19 mins), Smithfield (41 mins), The Liberties (40 mins), Temple Bar (26 mins), St Stephen's Green (29 mins), Merrion Square (16 mins)

Dart & South Western Commuter Train
Stop: Grand Canal Dock

Bus Routes to Grand Canal Dock: 47, 77A, 7A, C2, C3
Stops: Grand Canal Dock, Pearse Street, Grand Canal Quay, Grand Canal Street

BREWERY

Urban Brewing Tours

Best for:
Beer tasting.
■ plates.lift.slide

If you've had your fill of whiskey tasting or had enough of the finer 'black stuff', why not switch it up with a 40-minute brewery tour to learn how to craft the perfect beer? The tour includes a beer tasting session, and you can enjoy a selection of food, beer, wine, and cocktails afterwards. Tours run weekly on Wednesdays at 5pm and Saturdays at 3pm. We recommend booking in advance. Private tours for 6-15 people are also available for a more personalised experience.

MUSEUM — **EDITORS CHOICE**

EPIC The Irish Emigration Museum

Best for:
Discovering Ireland's history.
■ shift.lobby.blows

A must-visit for anyone fascinated by Ireland's history, EPIC The Irish Emigration Museum brings the story of Irish emigrants to life through a series of immersive exhibits and personal narratives. Visitors can explore the incredible journeys of those who left Ireland, uncover the reasons behind their emigration, and celebrate the remarkable achievements they made across the world. Housed in the historic CHQ building, the museum is fully accessible and open daily from 10am to 6.45pm (last entry at 5pm).

BOAT TOUR

Dublin Discovered Boat Tours

Best for:
A different view of the city.
■ later.belts.nation

Explore Dublin's landmarks by boat! This 45-minute tour departs daily from the Sean O'Casey Footbridge, offering a fresh perspective on the city with insightful commentary from expert guides. Sail along the River Liffey, passing under historic bridges and iconic sights. The journey continues through the Docklands, where modern architecture meets the city's maritime past. The tour operates seasonally, pausing from December to February, so be sure to check sailing times before visiting.

HISTORIC MUST-SEE — **EDITORS CHOICE**

The Jeanie Johnston: An Irish Famine Story

Best for:
Learning about Ireland's history.
■ proud.tester.layers

Step aboard and discover the dark history of Ireland's Great Famine (1845 -1852), which sadly claimed over a million lives. The 50-minute guided tour takes you around the ship, where you'll learn about the vessel's vital role in transporting Irish emigrants to North America and the conditions those travelling faced. It's such a moving tour, with very knowledgeable guides - we would highly recommend! Open daily year-round, the ship offers a glimpse into a key chapter of Ireland's past.

Famine Memorial Sculptures

HISTORIC SCULPTURE

Famine Memorial Sculptures

Best for:
A moment to reflect.

grin.robot.common

If you're in the area, it's worth taking a moment to visit the Famine Memorial on Customs House Quay. Officially called "Famine," the memorial, which was gifted to the city in 1997, honours the victims of the Great Famine, a tragic period in Ireland's history that led to a dramatic decrease in the country's population through death and emigration, claiming over a million lives. It's a place to pay tribute to those who suffered and were affected by this devastating period.

CITY TOUR

Secret Street Tours

Best for:
A different perspective on Dublin.

reform.phones.never

A non-profit social enterprise that offers walking tours of Dublin through the eyes of someone who has been affected by homelessness. The unique, friendly and powerful tours take guests through the city's major landmarks as well as discussing what life is like for those without homes. Tours can be booked online, with all money going directly to the guides and the operating costs of the programme. For those with accessibility needs, the 'South Side Tour' can be made wheelchair accessible, you'll need to email in advance.

The Jeanie Johnston

EPIC The Irish Emigration Museum

DOCK

Grand Canal Dock

Best for:
Shops, bars & entertainment.
ocean.swan.hook

Once one of the world's largest docks in the 18th century, Grand Canal Dock is now a thriving hub in Dublin. Lined with trendy bars, cafés, restaurants, and shops, it's the perfect spot to spend an afternoon while exploring nearby attractions. At its centre is Grand Canal Square, a striking urban space designed by architect Martha Schwartz. By day, it's home to leading financial and tech companies; by night, it transforms into a lively spot with a renowned theatre and nearby arena.

THEATRE

Bord Gáis Energy Theatre

Best for:
Popular theatre productions.
vision.scam.chop

A state-of-the-art venue designed by world-renowned architect Daniel Libeskind. The striking theatre is celebrated for its diverse range of performances, from operas and musicals to renowned touring productions. Nestled in the newly developed Grand Canal Dock area, it's the ideal place to enjoy an unforgettable evening of entertainment, especially after a delicious waterfront dinner. Tickets can be purchased through Ticketmaster, and wheelchair accessible seating is also available.

Bord Gáis Energy Theatre

ESCAPE ROOMS

Escape Boats

Best for:
A fun group activity.
broad.headed.apples

If you're looking for something unique to do with friends in the city, Dublin Escape Boats puts a fun spin on the classic escape room experience. Set on a moored boat, it's a great group activity where you can enjoy some friendly competition and put your problem-solving skills to the test! Choose between two themed rooms, SOS and Convicts, with each game lasting around an hour. Ticket prices vary based on the number of players. You'll need to pre-book in advance to secure your spot.

WATERSPORTS

Surfdock Watersports 10

Best for:
Outdoor watersport activities.
◼ lamps.send.privately

For those looking to add a little adventure to their city experience, Surf Dock has a variety of watersports to try. With activities like stand-up paddleboarding (SUP), kayaking, windsurfing, and wingsurfing, it's the perfect place to have a go at something a little different. Whether you're a beginner looking for lessons or planning a fun group outing, they've got several booking options available. It's a great way to enjoy the water and add a bit of adventure to your city break.

HISTORIC MUSIC VENUE

Windmill Lane Studio Tours 11

Best for:
Music-lovers.
◼ thanks.agreed.manage

Are you a music fan? Ever dreamed of mixing your own music or stepping into the shoes of a recording artist? Then a tour of the famous Windmill Lane Studios (established in 1978) should be on your list. Lasting around 60 minutes, the tour gives you a chance to learn how tracks are created, try your hand at mixing a session with a virtual band, and hear the stories of legendary artists who've recorded there. Plus, you might even bump into Cosmo, who is said to be the studio's famous ghost!

WALK & HISTORICAL LANDMARK

Great South Wall & Poolbeg Lighthouse 12

Best for:
Escaping the city.
◼ spin.echo.thick

Want to explore a different side of the city? Take a coastal walk to Poolbeg Lighthouse along the Great South Wall, which was the world's longest seawall when completed in 1731. Depending on how much time you have, you can opt for the shorter 3.4km route, which takes around 40 minutes, or the longer trail starting at Sandymount Strand, which takes a couple of hours. Whichever you choose, make sure you stay on the lookout for seals or dolphins, as this area is also part of the Dublin Bay Biosphere.

Poolbeg Lighthouse

WALKING TOUR
THE DOCKLANDS

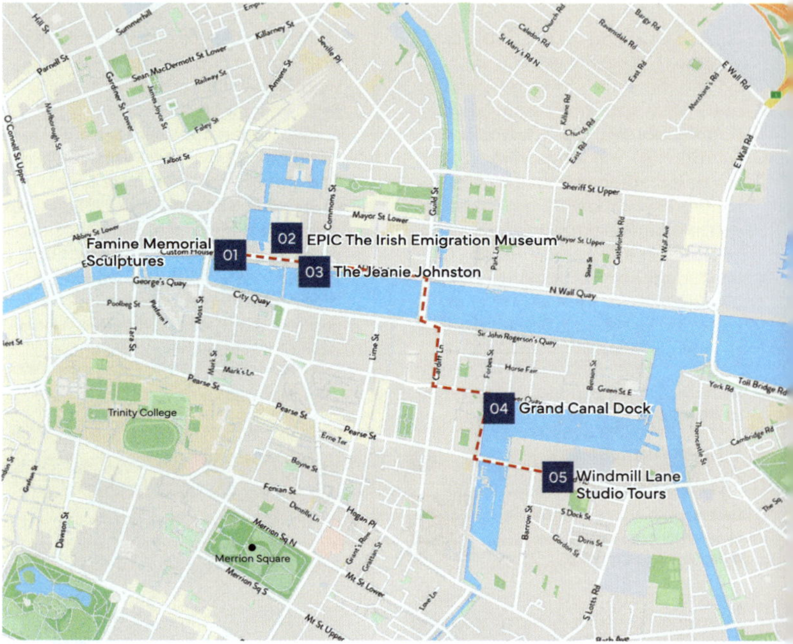

Begin your journey at the poignant Famine Sculptures along Dublin's River Liffey, reflecting on Ireland's rich yet tumultuous history. Stroll through the sleek, modern Docklands, admiring stunning architecture like the Samuel Beckett Bridge and Convention Centre. Pass Grand Canal Dock, often buzzing with activity, and marvel at colourful street art along the way. Conclude at Windmill Lane Recording Studios, the iconic music hub.

WALKING TOUR

TOTAL LENGTH: 1.8KM

DURATION: 25 MINS (NO STOPS)

TERRAIN: RELATIVELY FLAT COBBLES

STARTING POINT: FAMINE MEMORIAL SCULPTURES

END POINT: WINDMILL LANE STUDIOS

01
FAMINE MEMORIAL SCULPTURES

02
EPIC THE IRISH EMIGRATION MUSEUM

03
THE JEANIE JOHNSTON

04
GRAND CANAL DOCK

05
WINDMILL LANE STUDIO TOURS

DID YOU KNOW?

Windmill Lane Recording Studios, located in Dublin's Docklands, has been a pivotal part of Ireland's music scene since 1978. Famous for hosting iconic bands like U2, it played a key role in recording some of their most legendary albums, including The Joshua Tree. The studios have also welcomed international artists like David Bowie and The Cranberries. Windmill Lane's rich history in shaping global music is celebrated throughout the fascinating studio tours.

TIME FOR A BREAK?

Worked up an appetite? Head to **Sprout & Co,** offering nutritious bowls of goodness, tasty wraps, and delicious sides. It's an ideal place to stop whilst you're on the go.

MEMORABLE MOMENT:

A journey through history, exploring Dublin's Docklands.

BY NO FUSS TRAVEL EDITOR, DANI MAZUR

With the sun shining down across Dublin, we thought it would be the perfect day to visit the Docklands and soak up the riverside views. Before hitting the museums, our first stop was 'As One' for breakfast. I loved it here and have to say, it felt like every ingredient on your plate had been carefully considered, not your standard fry-up that's for sure!

Afterwards, we hit the museums, starting with the EPIC The Irish Emigration Museum. It's worth a trip to the Docklands for this alone! A series of immersive rooms tell emigration stories, many of which were incredibly moving. We also learned more about Ireland's influence on music, dance, and art, which is truly global. You can even try your hand at Irish dancing if you're not too shy! While you're here, you'll get your own passport to stamp as you venture to the different areas of the museum – this was surprisingly satisfying to tick off and a nice interactive feature.

From here, we booked a tour of the Jeanie Johnston ship, which is docked right outside the EPIC Museum. Personally, this was one of the

> **"** The stories of resilience left a lasting impression. Our guide, Steven, brought these powerful accounts to life with his exceptional storytelling and in-depth knowledge. **"**

highlights of the trip. I wasn't entirely sure what to expect, but learning about the Irish famine and the personal stories of those who embarked on this journey was truly eye-opening. The harsh conditions they endured were unimaginable, yet the stories of resilience left a lasting impression. Our guide, Steven, brought these powerful accounts to life with his exceptional storytelling and in-depth knowledge.

If you find yourself in the area, I highly recommend this tour – it's certainly worth dedicating an hour of your time. Afterwards, we headed to the Grand Canal Dock to enjoy some lunch, following a busy yet insightful morning.

Ireland Never Leaves You

ROOFTOP RESTAURANT

Ryleigh's Rooftop Steakhouse

▪ basic.noon.also

Found on the 6th floor of The Mayson hotel, this stylish restaurant offers an elevated dining experience whether you're looking for breakfast, lunch or dinner. Overlooking the River Liffey, it provides stunning panoramic views of Dublin, so enjoy a cocktail whilst taking in the views. Open daily.

BOAT RESTAURANT & BAR

MV Cill Airne

▪ pills.appeal.energetic

Fancy dinner on a boat? Head to Dublin's unique floating restaurant and bar on the River Liffey. Enjoy a meal in Quay 16 Restaurant serving classic dishes or relax with a drink (or two) at the Blue River Bistro Bar on the upper deck, offering stunning views of the river.

HEALTHY BOWLS & BITES

Sprout & Co Campshires

▪ phones.visual.match

Looking for a healthy lunch option? Well, this is the place, offering nutritious bowls of goodness, tasty wraps, and delicious sides. The ideal spot if you're on the go and wanting to grab a quick bite to eat. Their produce is all local and seasonal, some even grown at their own farm!

As One

BREAKFAST & BRUNCH CAFÉ

As One

▪ renew.liver.toys

Dedicated to creating "food with purpose," this neighbourhood brunch spot serves up dishes made with locally sourced and thoughtfully selected ingredients. Their menu features healthy options like smoked salmon muffins and flavourful risottos, designed to nourish.

BREAKFAST & BRUNCH CAFÉ — 17

3fe Gertrude

senior.suffice.online

A café known for its top-quality coffee and relaxed atmosphere. Serving specialty brews from 3fe alongside fresh pastries and delicious brunch options, from porridge and pancakes to avocado toast. 3fe Gertrude is a firm favourite among both locals and visitors in the area.

CASUAL PUB — 18

The Storyteller

camp.achieving.icons

A casual welcoming pub, serving hearty comfort food classics like buffalo wings, fish finger sandwiches, and more. It's the ideal spot to unwind with a drink in hand, whether you're catching up with friends or enjoying a laid-back evening listening to live music.

BREAKFAST & BRUNCH CAFÉ — 19

Herbstreet

snake.chill.shaped

A family-owned restaurant that's perfect for any time of day. Whether you're stopping by for breakfast, lunch, or dinner, you'll find something delicious to enjoy. Overlooking the waterfront, it's a convenient and relaxing spot to refuel during a day of sightseeing.

HEALTHY BITES & BOWLS — 20

Nutbutter Grand Canal Dock

adjust.sunk.spots

Think fresh, healthy, and incredibly tasty with a Californian twist at this casual lunch and dinner spot, where every ingredient is thoughtfully chosen. From tacos and rice bowls to hearty seasonal specials, there's something for every taste, including plenty of veggie and vegan options.

BAKERY & CAFÉ — 21

Il Valentino Bakery & Café

trend.monkey.clown

If you're looking for a quick lunch, this bakery serves up a selection of savoury pizzas and sandwiches, alongside irresistible sweet treats like pastries, cakes, and not to forget cream-filled eclairs! Plus, they're all made by-hand, slow proved and freshly baked on-site.

MEDITERRANEAN INSPIRED — 22

Charlotte Quay

abode.crest.roof

Charlotte Quay is a vibrant restaurant and bar known for it's a lively atmosphere. Delivering Mediterranean-inspired dishes, they aim to source the finest Irish produce. The dedicated pre-theatre menu also makes it a great option for dinner before heading to a show.

THE DOCKLANDS | WHERE TO EAT & DRINK

203

FINE-DINING ITALIAN (23)

Osteria Lucio

▪ flesh.struck.term

A contemporary fine-dining Italian restaurant owned by Michelin-starred chef Ross Lewis and friend Luciano Tona. Enjoy Italian classics, freshly made pasta and hand-selected wines. A perfect spot for a romantic evening or celebrating a special occasion.

JAPANESE (24)

YOI Ramen

▪ poem.actors.yarn

A small cosy Japanese restaurant specialising in ramen, poke bowls, and freshly made sushi. With a focus on quality ingredients and traditional techniques, Yoi Ramen offers an authentic, casual dining experience. Reservations can be made via phone call only (016687959).

Bites by kwanghi

AMERICAN-STYLE COMFORT FOOD (25)

Mackenzie's

▪ cage.shunts.trying

A spot for American-style comfort food, Mackenzie's serves up everything from pizza, sandwiches and burgers to juicy steaks. Don't miss their delicious brunch options, including pancakes and French toast - what's not to like?! Kid's menus are available.

BAR & RESTAURANT (26)

Allta

▪ went.yards.fall

A sophisticated restaurant and bar with a menu to match, featuring innovative dishes, including roast potato ice cream, believe it or not! So, if you're wanting to taste something that is a little out of the ordinary then this is the place for you. They also have a separate vegetarian menu.

ASIAN STREET FOOD (27)

Bites by Kwanghi

▪ shorts.arch.ports

Known for award-winning Asian street food with a modern twist, Bites by Kwanghi offers everything from bao buns to katsu curry to ramen and even Asian style tacos! Also, don't miss the sushi - they've got plenty of delicious options to choose from!

As One

HOTEL 28

The Gibson Hotel

+353(0) 1 681 5000

boat.broom.amuse

This modern hotel offers panoramic views of Dublin Port and is just steps from the 3Arena. You can also relax with a drink on the open bar terrace and soak up those amazing city views! They also have an on-site restaurant and gym.

HOTEL 29

The Mayson Dublin

+353 1 2457900

closes.making.onion

A modern boutique hotel with luxurious rooms, situated just moments from Dublin's top attractions, shops, restaurants, and bars. For a special stay (and hefty price) you can enjoy one of the city's best penthouse suites with stunning rooftop views.

HOTEL 30

The Samuel Hotel

+353 1 556 7750

woes.snail.eggs

Located at Spencer Place, this hotel offers a range of deluxe modern rooms. With a chic bar and brasserie-style restaurant, it's the perfect spot for dining. Ideally located near the 3Arena, it's a great choice for show-goers.

HOTEL 31

The Spencer Hotel

+353 1 433 8800

steep.shirt.rests

The Spencer Hotel is the place to stay if you're looking to unwind after hours on your feet exploring Dublin. Guests of the hotel have access to the on-site Health Club that includes a sauna, steam room and jacuzzi – bliss!

HOTEL 32

Hilton Garden Inn Dublin City Centre

+353 1 854 1500

crown.dime.print

Located next to the EPIC Museum, the hotel offers spacious rooms for a comfortable stay. Connolly Station is a 2-minute walk away, plus there's a tram stop and sightseeing tour stop just outside, ideally positioned for easy access to Dublin's attractions.

HOTEL 33

The Ferryman Townhouse

+353 (1) 671 7053

spits.lows.chief

The ideal place to stay if you are visiting for a fun-filled weekend getaway! Situated in two beautifully restored Georgian buildings, it offers modern, good-value rooms perched above a lively pub. If you're after relaxation, this might not be the one for you.

HOTEL 34

Clayton Hotel Cardiff Lane

+353 1 643 9500

dwell.slim.lakes

Conveniently located near the Bord Gáis Energy Theatre and Dublin's Docklands, this stylish hotel offers a variety of room options. Guests can also enjoy the added perk of an indoor pool, a fully equipped fitness centre, and an on-site restaurant.

HOTEL 35

Anantara The Marker Hotel

+353 1 687 5100

carry.dame.cove

If you want to experience pure luxury during your trip, this modern 5-star hotel tops the list. Overlooking Grand Canal Square, it features a spa with a 23-metre infinity pool, a rooftop bar offering 360° city views and an award-winning restaurant.

HOTEL 36

Maldron Hotel Pearse Street

+353 1 670 3666

lease.boats.frozen

This 4-star hotel has a range of stylish family and executive rooms. Maldron Hotel is ideally located, just a 5-minute walk from Grand Canal Dock and the iconic Bord Gáis Energy Theatre, plus a 15-minute stroll to O'Connell Street.

Anantara The Marker Hotel

HOTEL 37

Schoolhouse Hotel & GastroBar

+353 1 667 5014

circle.yarn.assist

Tucked away beside the canal, this quaint boutique hotel offers cosy, character-filled rooms providing a peaceful retreat from the city chaos. Guests can unwind in the open courtyard or enjoy some old-school dishes at the on-site gastropub.

HOTEL 38

Grand Canal Hotel

+353 (0) 164 61000

handy.guides.bless

This family-run hotel, located near key attractions in the area, offers modern and comfortable rooms. It's also a short walk from Grand Canal Dart Station and 15 minutes from the city centre - perfect for exploring Dublin!

207

Beyond the City

Step away from the city's hustle and bustle and spend a day or two discovering the treasures beyond Dublin's centre. From stunning beaches to scenic mountain views, the surrounding area offers a wealth of attractions waiting to be explored.

BEYOND THE CITY:
There's more to Dublin than just the city centre!

It's entirely understandable that most first-time visitors to Dublin tend to stay within a mile or two of Temple Bar. However, once you step away from the city centre's vibrant hustle and bustle, you'll find a wealth of remarkable and often overlooked locations to explore. From stunning beaches to scenic mountain landscapes, the areas surrounding Dublin are brimming with hidden gems. If you have an extra day in the city or if you've visited before and are eager to uncover something new, venture beyond the heart of Dublin – you certainly won't be disappointed.

TOP 5 THINGS TO SEE & DO

01
MALAHIDE

02
HOWTH

03
DOLLYMOUNT STRAND BEACH

04
DALKEY & DALKEY ISLAND

05
KILLINEY BEACH

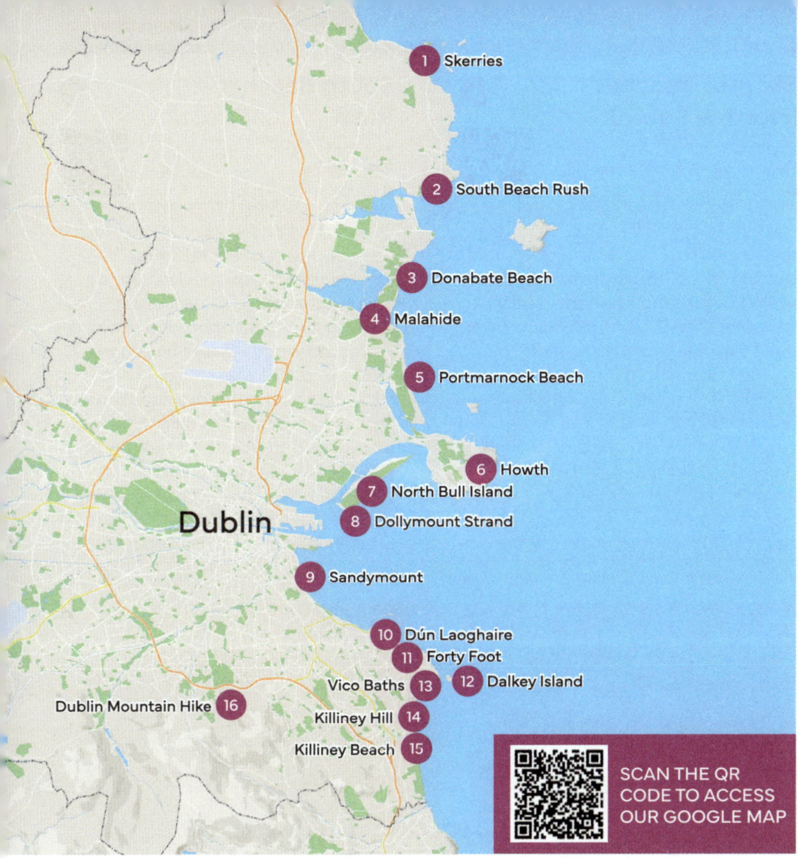

Map locations:
1. Skerries
2. South Beach Rush
3. Donabate Beach
4. Malahide
5. Portmarnock Beach
6. Howth
7. North Bull Island
8. Dollymount Strand
9. Sandymount
10. Dún Laoghaire
11. Forty Foot
12. Dalkey Island
13. Vico Baths
14. Killiney Hill
15. Killiney Beach
16. Dublin Mountain Hike

SCAN THE QR CODE TO ACCESS OUR GOOGLE MAP

GETTING HERE

 Dart Train
Travel between Howth and Killiney

 Northern Commuter Train
Travel north of Howth to Malahide, Donabate, Rush and Skerries

 Bus Route: 130
Travel to North Bull Island

BEYOND THE CITY

BEACH

Skerries Beaches (North & South) ❶

Best for:
Family-friendly beach days.

october.otters.stroll

Skerries beaches (North and South) are located approx. 31-miles North of Dublin city centre and sit either side of Red Island. You'll find the North Beach next to Skerries Harbour. From the 2.5km South Beach stretch you can see across to the three nearby islands; Shenick Island, Colt Island and St Patrick's Island. There are kayak tours which take you to each island. Irish Rail run regular trains from Dublin Pearse Station to Skerries (46-minute journey), followed by an approx. 20-minute walk to the beach.

BEACH **LOCALS CHOICE**

South Beach Rush ❷

Best for:
Beach walks.

claims.screamed.waxer

Located in the seaside town of Rush, this popular spot stretches for 2.4 km. The sandy beach is backed by a well-established dune system, making it an ideal spot for a relaxing walk, and was awarded Blue Flag status in 2022. To the north, there is a rocky headland that provides some shelter to the beach, while the southern end is particularly popular with kite surfers. To reach South Beach, take the Northern Commuter Train to Rush & Lusk, where you'll have a 50-minute walk or a short taxi ride.

Skerries

BEACH

Donabate Beach (Balcarrick Beach)

Best for:
Sea dipping & rock pooling.
▪ avoidable.roaming.bond

Situated approx. 23-miles North of Dublin city centre, Donabate is ideal if you're looking for a dip in the sea, a spot of rock pooling or a scenic dog walk *(please note dogs must be kept on leads)*. The sandy beach stretches for 3km and has incredible views over to Lambay Island, Howth and Malahide. Irish Rail trains run regularly from Dublin Connolly Station to Donabate (24-minute journey), its then an approx. 35-minute walk from the station to the beach (or a 5-minute taxi ride).

VILLAGE

Malahide

Best for:
Beach walks & castle visits.
▪ drain.candles.neon

Reachable via a 20-minute train ride from the city, Malahide is a coastal village filled with cobbled streets, boutiques, cafés and pubs. It's home to the Malahide Castle & Gardens estate, which offers 260-acres of parkland to explore. Malahide Beach is ideal for a scenic walk (swimming is not recommended due to the strong and unpredictable tidal currents). Fancy a longer walk? Take the 4km trail along the Coastal Route to Portmarnock, an elevated path with parkland on one side and the sea on the other.

BEACH

Portmarnock Beach (Velvet Strand)

Best for:
Swimming & windsurfing.
▪ linked.make.entertainer

Portmarnock Beach (otherwise known as Velvet Strand due to its silky-smooth sand), served as a makeshift runway back in 1930 for Australian pilot Charles Kingsford Smith (you'll find an aviation themed monument next to the beach). Reachable via a 25-minute train journey, followed by an approx. 35-minute walk from the station to the beach, the 5km stretch of sand offers scenic views across to Ireland's Eye and Howth. It's the ideal spot for a paddle with calm, shallow waters and is also popular with kite surfers and windsurfers.

VILLAGE

Howth

Best for:
Stunning cliffside walk & beaches.
▪ breathless.toils.overpriced

A picturesque coastal village, home to a scenic harbour, a castle, and four beaches. It's the ideal place to explore if you're a keen walker— the Howth Cliff Walk is arguably the best reason to visit. There are several routes along the wildflower-covered sea cliffs, and we'd recommend walking out to the 1814 Baily Lighthouse. Keep your eyes peeled for seals, as they often frequent the coastline here. Howth is easily reachable by train, approximately a 30-minute ride from the city centre. Be sure to try some fresh seafood here!

BEYOND THE CITY

Howth Lighthouse

NATURE RESERVE & BEACH

North Bull Island

Best for:
Bird spotting.
cared.email.first

Inhabited only by birds and wildlife, in the 1930's North Bull Island was the first official bird sanctuary in the country and in 1981 it achieved status as a UNESCO Biosphere Reserve due to its rare habitats and species. To reach the island you'll want to hop on the Route 130 bus from the city, which will take around 20-minutes. The long and thin island is great scenic walks but be sure to wrap up as it's known to have strong winds all year round. We stopped for a coffee and toastie at the 'Happy Out' café, which we would recommend.

BEACH

Dollymount Strand Beach

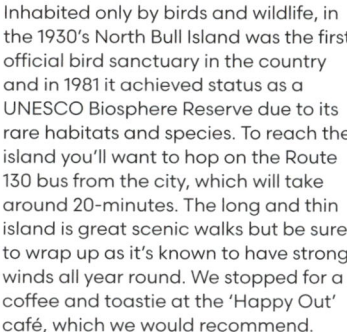

Best for:
Swimming, walking & watersports.
blank.enhancement.risks

Situated on North Bull Island, this vast sandy beach stretches the full 3-mile length of the island. Enjoy striking views over Dublin Bay, the Howth Peninsula and the Poolbeg Chimneys. It's a popular spot for dog-walkers, swimmers, paddleboarders and kite-surfers. We spotted a lot of people braving the cold water, in fact, there were a lot taking advantage of the dedicated bathing shelters along the Bull Wall. Look out for birds nesting in the sand dunes, and if you're lucky you might spot a seal at the northern end of the beach.

BEACH

Sandymount Strand Beach

Best for:
Beach walks with a view.
surely.ranked.blend

Sandymount Strand is the closest beach to the city centre and is part of the Dublin Bay Biosphere Reserve. The dog-friendly beach has a promenade which runs the full coast road, with gorgeous views across to Dun Laoghaire, Howth and the Poolbeg Lighthouse. It's also home to one of the Martello Towers *(built in the early 1800s to protect the area from Napoleonic invasion)*, as well as the Cailín Bán sculpture by Mexican artist Sebastian. If you're looking for a bite to eat, then head to Sandymount Green (approx. 5-minute walk).

HARBOUR TOWN

Dún Laoghaire

Best for:
Boat trips, walks & more.
hers.sentences.jelly

This lively harbour town sits 14km southeast of Dublin and is a popular spot for watersports. Cruises out to Howth are on offer, take a 75-minute trip out past Dalkey Island, Ireland's Eye and Lambay Island, where you might spot the herd of resident wallabies (yes, wallabies). Dún Laoghaire's harbour is encircled by two pier walls (East and West), each with a lighthouse. The People's Park is home to the Victorian gatehouse, fountains, tea rooms, children's playground and a fragrant garden for the blind with a safe walking trail.

BEYOND THE CITY

215

BEYOND THE CITY

WILD SWIMMING SPOT

Forty Foot (11)

Best for:
Wild swimming.

caviar.breeds.futuristic

Arguably one of the most famous places to take a dip in Dublin, you'll find Forty Foot at the tip of Dublin Bay in Sandycove. Although it is now a popular spot amongst locals, it was once a male-only bathing area - that was until a group of women's equality activists took a leap into the sea in 1974. Since then, women and children have been welcome to swim here. As with anytime you enter the open water, it's important to exercise caution. Always follow water safety guidelines and be aware of hidden rocks.

TOWN & ISLAND

Dalkey & Dalkey Island (12)

Best for: Exploring a posh coastal town with picturesque parks.

jinxed.imperious.fool

Dalkey is one of Dublin's most affluent areas *(home to famous faces such as U2's Bono)*. Explore the coastal town's narrow streets, filled with shops. Discover Dalkey Castle *(its scenic views are a reason to visit)*, or Sorrento Park and Dillon's Park, which both offer gorgeous viewpoints over the coast and out to Dalkey Island. The 25-acre, uninhabited Dalkey Island lies approx. 300 metres off the coastline, and can be explored via boat or kayak. Take the DART train line from the city centre, reaching Dalkey will take around 30-minutes.

WILD SWIMMING SPOT

Vico Baths (13)

Best for:
A cold dip.

pegged.suspicions.sadness

Located in-between Dalkey and Killiney (and only accessible through a small gap in a wall on Vico Road) you'll find one of the most popular swimming spots in Dublin and possibly the most scenic – especially at sunrise, when you can watch the golden glow over the Dublin Mountains. There's also a seawater pool to escape the sometimes-choppy waters. Enjoy a dip in the Irish Sea but please take caution if entering the cold and rocky waters, diving is NOT advised.

Vico Baths

PARK & VIEWPOINT

Killiney Hill

Best for:
Walks with spectacular views.
blossom.carriage.bankers

Located within the small Killiney Hill Park, Killiney Hill stands 153 meters high and is crowned by an obelisk monument and a pyramid *(which locals refer to as the 'Wishing Stone')*. You'll be treated to spectacular views across Dublin and the surrounding areas, including the Wicklow Mountains, Bray Head, and the Irish Sea. Take the DART train from the city centre to Killiney station (next to the beach); from there, it takes approximately 15 minutes to reach the Killiney Hill viewpoint.

Dalkey Island

BEACH

Killiney Beach

Best for:
Sea dipping & dog walking.
trade.blackboard.overreact

This pebbled beach is an ideal spot for swimming and bathing. Stretching around 2.5km in length it's also a great place for a stroll, with gorgeous views across to Dalkey Island, Sorrento Terrace and Bray Head. Dogs are welcome but must be kept on leads. Finish off with a coffee from Fred and Nancys food truck, located on the northside of the beach. You'll want to jump on an approx. 40-minute train to reach Killiney station, the station is conveniently located next to the seafront, so you won't have far to walk from there.

MOUNTAINS

Dublin Mountains Hike

Best for:
Keen hikers.
chain.dated.hush

Explore a different side to the city with a scenic Dublin Mountain hike. The Ticknock hike will take around 1.5-2.5 hours depending on your fitness levels and is a perfect way to escape the hustle and bustle of the city. Once you reach the top, you'll have endless views over Dublin. You might need to pencil in some extra time just to soak up the epic views! Did you know that despite the name, the Dublin Mountains aren't actually mountains? In fact, they are technically classed as hills!

MEMORABLE MOMENT:

A sunny (yet very windy) visit to North Bull Island!

BY NO FUSS TRAVEL EDITOR, LAURA MAYES

We'd not long arrived at Dublin port *(which can be seen opposite the island)* when we decided to make a lunch stop and stretch our legs on North Bull Island. We headed for the container café 'Happy Out' to grab a coffee *(or hot chocolate, in my case)* and a toastie, which was delicious by the way. After that, we took a stroll down the Bull Wall, where we observed people taking a dip in the cold Irish Sea *(brave!)* from the designated swimming shelters. We continued on to the island's beach, Dollymount Strand. Even in the August sunshine, it was fairly windy and chilly, so be sure to wrap up warm if you're planning a walk here. If you've had your fill of the city, North Bull Island is only a short distance from the centre, making it the perfect place to escape. Reconnect with nature, feel the wind in your hair, breathe in the fresh sea air, and listen to the birds gliding above you – my idea of heaven!

> **❝** If you've had your fill of the city, North Bull Island is only a short distance from the centre, making it the perfect place to escape. Feel the wind in your hair, breathe in the fresh sea air, and listen to the birds gliding above you – heavenly! **❞**

SEAFOOD 17

Stoop Your Head (Skerries)

nodded.discharges.individually

Stoop Your Head has been serving the finest seafood in the coastal town of Skerries for over 50 years. Sat on the only west-facing harbour on Ireland's east coast, guests can enjoy amazing waterfront views whilst digging into hearty meals like fresh cod frittè and the eatery's famous seafood chowder.

CAFÉ 18

Olive Café & Deli (Skerries)

normality.rejoining.central

Olive Café & Deli is a family-run eatery that delivers top-quality taste, service and community spirit. Grab a cup of coffee sourced from a local micro-roastery, a spot of lunch or even a full food box, all perfect for a picnic down on South Beach, just a three-minute walk away.

BRASSERIE 19

The Shoreline Bar & Bistro (Donabate)

generic.owned.sprays

Take in the stunning sea views of Lambay Island and Dublin Bay as you dine out in the Shoreline Bar & Bistro – located within the Shoreline Hotel. Pre-booking is advised on weekends and holidays, with breakfast, lunch and dinner available 7-days a week – they even offer afternoon tea.

CAFÉ 20

Déjà Vu (Malahide)

conclude.quibble.careless

Bringing a taste of France to the coastal village of Malahide, Déjà Vu is a Parisian-inspired café that serves up breakfast and lunch 7-days a week. Guests enjoy expertly brewed coffee, freshly baked pastries and a menu chockablock with locally sourced and French-inspired dishes.

PAKISTANI 21

Kajjal (Malahide)

uniform.rents.feathers

Kajjal delivers mouth-watering Pakistani and Middle Eastern flavours in a relaxed, modern setting. With indoor and outdoor seating, plus wide-ranging dishes from creamy chicken tikka masala to spicy prawn jalfrezi, it's a spot sure to please all palates! They're open Wednesday to Sunday.

Kajjal (Malahide)

ITALIAN

That's Amore (Malahide)

■ manager.multiple.rare

"When the moon hits your eye, it's time for pizza pie at That's Amore..." That's the unofficial (entirely made up by us) anthem of That's Amore in Malahide. Founded in 2004, this eatery hits all the Italian comfort dishes, from big ol' bowls of carbonara to rich aubergine parmigiana.

INDIAN

Jaipur (Malahide)

■ minerals.pickles.rooster

Consistently featured in top restaurant guides, Jaipur Malahide has brought the experience of Indian fine dining to Ireland. Set in a Georgian basement, its comfy interior and open floor seating make for a great environment to dig into the many (it's a big menu) flavourful dishes.

EUROPEAN

McGoverns Restaurant (Malahide)

■ property.instead.troubled

McGovern's Restaurant serves expertly crafted Irish and European cuisine in a friendly, casual set up. Known for its fresh, locally sourced ingredients, standout seafood dishes and welcoming staff, it's an excellent option for some great food surrounded by good people.

GRILL HOUSE & PIZZA BAR

Scotch Bonnet (Malahide)

■ cycled.electric.racks

Known for their mouthwatering ribs, wings and pizzas – as well as a selection of cocktails. If you're in Malahide and fancy a meaty meal, Scotch Bonnet is the place. They also offer a takeaway menu. Please note that they are closed on Monday's and Tuesday's.

PUB

O'Connells Pub & Restaurant (Howth)

■ gazer.merrier.rehearsals

O'Connells has combined the Irish traditions of good food, plenty of drinks and live music since 2012. The owner wanted to create a place that would feel like a home away from home, with comfy seats and great views out to Lambay Island and Ireland's Eye – mission accomplished, we say!

SEAFOOD

Aqua Restaurant (Howth)

■ desolation.fatigued.cartoons

Aqua Restaurant is a top choice for seafood lovers, cooking up award-winning dishes made with the freshest local ingredients. With its chic interiors and unbeatable sea views, it's a great option for special occasions or those who like to dine with a view!

CAFÉ — EDITORS CHOICE

Happy Out (North Bull Island)

help.kinks.depend

Starting out as a simple shipping container at the end of the Bull Wall, Happy Out is the go-to locale for delicious sandwiches, great coffee, tasty breakfast bits, pastries and sweet cakes. Open all year round, make sure to get there before 3pm if you're after their famed toasties!

BURGERS

BuJo Sandymount

draw.period.thick

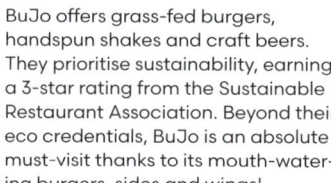

BuJo offers grass-fed burgers, handspun shakes and craft beers. They prioritise sustainability, earning a 3-star rating from the Sustainable Restaurant Association. Beyond their eco credentials, BuJo is an absolute must-visit thanks to its mouth-watering burgers, sides and wings!

ASIAN

Kyoto Asian Street Food (Dún Laoghaire)

gifted.puff.daring

Kyoto Asian Street Food delivers bold, authentic flavours with a menu covering everything from Thai curries, noodle stir-fries and handmade dumplings. A good shout for a casual meal or takeaway, it's all about fresh ingredients, generous portions and flavour-packed dishes here.

BRASSERIE

Casper & Giumbini's (Dún Laoghaire)

glory.milk.moved

A contemporary Irish brasserie that serves fresh seafood, premium char-grilled steaks and trademark burgers. Not to be left out, the eatery also has its own vegan and veggie menu. Found on Dún Laoghaire's near promenade, it's perfect for a pre-or post-meal stroll along the harbour.

EUROPEAN

Hartley's (Dún Laoghaire)

dish.kinds.empty

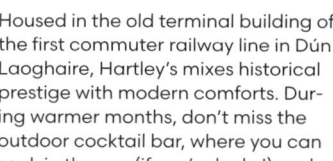

Housed in the old terminal building of the first commuter railway line in Dún Laoghaire, Hartley's mixes historical prestige with modern comforts. During warmer months, don't miss the outdoor cocktail bar, where you can soak in the sun (if you're lucky!) and enjoy the views of the harbour.

PIZZA

Zero Zero Pizza (Dún Laoghaire)

clay.dips.props

Zero Zero serves real-deal Neapolitan-style pizzas with expertly blistered crusts straight from their traditional wood-fired oven. Get ready for fresh ingredients, friendly service and pizza so good you'll be back for seconds. To sum up in five words: simple, satisfying and seriously tasty!

Happy Out (North Bull Island)

BAR

McLoughlin's Bar
(Dún Laoghaire)

laws.woods.piano

A proper Irish watering hole that ticks off all the boxes, McLoughlin's Bar is home to friendly locals, live music sessions and classic pub grub. Whether you're after a relaxed meal or a lively night of music, swing by for great craic, good food and a pint or two.

ITALIAN

Benito's Restaurant
(Dalkey)

reside.nips.section

Benito's brings rustic Italian dining to the table with wood-fired pizzas, homemade pasta and fresh seafood. Pair that with a cracking wine list, friendly service and cosy atmosphere, and you've got the perfect spot for a relaxed meal after a day of sightseeing.

INDIAN

Jaipur
(Dalkey)

swings.passing.cliffs

A polished but unpretentious place to enjoy out-of-this-world Indian dishes, Jaipur Dalkey was built on a love for food and art. Its walls are adorned with artwork from around the world, while its menu will have you transported across the globe to the streets of India!

LOCALS CHOICE

"Pretty Dalkey, south of the city, is the playground of Ireland's rich and famous, and **DeVille's**, at its heart, sits somewhere between a pub and a bistro, serving locally sourced oysters, lamb, scallops and steaks."

LOCAL WRITER, JAMES HENDICOTT

FRENCH — LOCALS CHOICE

DeVille's
(Dalkey)

bridges.fronts.knee

Born out of a love of food and the ceremony of dining out, DeVille's brings hearty bistro classics with a French twist. Expect char-grilled Irish steaks, fresh seafood and signature burgers, alongside crafted cocktails, fine wines and friendly service to boot.

WORLD CUISINE

Nova Restaurant
(Dalkey)

tuxedos.activism.highlander

If you're in one of those moods when you can't settle on what kind of food you fancy, Nova Restaurant has you covered. Serving dishes from around the world, including Mexican, Italian and American, it's the ideal spot to satisfy any craving. They're closed on Mondays.

ITALIAN  39

Ragazzi Restaurant (Dalkey)

replies.sacrificed.bathrobes

A busy little bistro not far from the coast, Ragazzi has mastered thin-crust pizza, fresh pasta and sweet desserts. With its warm atmosphere and real Italian flavours, it's a great option for those looking for a taste of the Mediterranean during their trip. They're closed Mondays and Tuesdays.

SEAFOOD RESTAURANT 40

Guinea Pig (Dalkey)

pieced.dependents.devalued

Founded in 1957, and now owned by French chef Jérôme Fernandes, Guinea Pig prides itself on its locally sourced fresh fish, shellfish, beef and lamb, as well as offering an extensive vegetarian menu. Dinner is available Wednesday - Sunday from 5.30pm and lunch on Sunday's from 12pm.

PUB 41

Finnegan's of Dalkey

rang.messed.autocratic

A pub now drenched in Dublin lore, Finnegan's of Dalkey first opened its doors back in 1970. In its over 50-year history, the pub has attracted some of Ireland's most famous faces, including U2's Bono who declared the former owner as the 'uncrowned king of Dalkey'.

FOOD & DRINK TRUCK 42

Fred and Nancy's (Killiney Beach)

fussed.acceleration.centurion

Proud to be serving some of 'life's simple pleasures', Fred and Nancy's is a small food truck found right on Killiney Bay Beach. There's nothing quite like grabbing a sandwich, sweet treat or hot drink, finding a comfy spot on the beach and watching the waves roll by.

PUB 43

Johnnie Fox's Pub (Dublin Mountains)

gasped.elevates.timbered

Taking the crown of 'Ireland's Highest Pub', Johnnie Fox's can be found in the village of Glencullen, surrounded by the Dublin Mountains. Drink, dine and be endlessly entertained, with traditional Irish tunes and dancing a staple at the pub's ticketed 'Hooley Show'. They run a shuttle bus from Dublin city centre.

Johnnie Fox's Pub

HOTEL 44

Grand Hotel Malahide

+353 1 845 0000

crush.nuance.poster

Less than 20 minutes from Dublin Airport, this hotel offers 203 luxurious rooms and complimentary access to its award-winning health club, complete with a gym, pool and spa – excellent for unwinding after a flight or a busy few days exploring the city.

HOTEL 45

Portmarnock Resort & Jameson Golf Links

+353 1 846 0611

grower.amused.cookies

If you're looking to hit the links during your trip, a stay here offers the perfect excuse! The historic home of the Jameson whiskey dynasty, the hotel provides its guests with a spa, three dining options and 18 holes of uninterrupted golfing bliss.

GUESTHOUSE 46

King Sitric Guesthouse

+353 1 832 5235

artery.clued.glancing

Offering excellent views across the beautiful Balscadden Bay, King Sitric Guesthouse is a great choice for those looking to stay away from the crowds and enjoy some fresh sea air! Dogs are welcome, as long as they don't bark throughout the night.

HOTEL  47

Clontarf Castle Hotel

+353 1 833 2321

towers.axed.cabin

Clontarf Castle Hotel nails the balance between historic significance and modern comfort. Think plush rooms and top-notch dining, all inside an impressive castle – just a short trip north of the city centre. They have on-site bar and dining options.

HOTEL 48

Sandymount Hotel

+353 1 614 2000

nodded.school.pokers

Sandymount Hotel is Dublin's oldest independent family-run hotel that dates back over 250 years. With 187 luxurious rooms, a fitness suite and a location just 20 minutes from the city centre via the DART, you can't go wrong with a stay here.

BED & BREAKFAST 49

Aberdeen Lodge

+353 1 283 8155

apron.fully.scare

A beautiful Victorian villa, offering en-suite rooms and breakfast. Family-run and full of warmth, it's ideally located just minutes from Sandymount Strand beach and a short 15-minute trip from the city. Dogs are welcome for an additional €20.

HOTEL

 50

Royal Marine Hotel

+353 1 230 0030

books.loops.ledge

A historical 4-star hotel dating back to 1828, the Royal Marine Hotel is one of Dún Laoghaire's most iconic landmarks. This is the place to stay if you're looking to relax, with its Sansana Spa and Pier Health Club available to guests.

HOTEL

 51

Haddington House

+353 1 280 1810

closet.waving.whites

Originally four Victorian townhouses, Haddington House was converted into a hotel during the 1950s. Overlooking Dún Laoghaire harbour, there are rooms to suit different budgets, a parlour to relax in and a critically acclaimed on-site restaurant to dine in.

HOTEL

 52

Fitzpatrick Castle Hotel

+353 1 230 5400

sludgy.recoils.overdone

Fitzpatrick Castle Hotel combines the classiness of an 18th-century castle with all the modern comforts you can need. Expect cosy rooms, a 20m pool, a sauna, incredible dining options and panoramic views over Dublin Bay and beyond!

Dún Laoghaire Harbour

DAY TRIPS
FROM DUBLIN CITY

Looking to elevate your Dublin experience and explore some of Ireland's other iconic destinations? We've curated a selection of must-visit day trips that are sure to enhance your Irish adventure.

GIANT'S CAUSEWAY & BELFAST CITY
Length of trip: 12 hours

Venture into Northern Ireland on this bus tour where you'll explore Northern Ireland's dramatic coastline. With stops at the iconic Giant's Causeway, the Dark Hedges (a Game of Thrones fan favourite) and Dunluce Castle, finished with a stop off in Belfast City.

Belfast

NEWGRANGE & THE BOYNE VALLEY
Length of trip: 8 hours

Explore the UNESCO-listed Boyne Valley as you travel through Co. Louth and Co. Meath. The day trip includes visits to the Newgrange Monument, Bru Na Boinne, the Battle of the Boyne Visitor Centre, and Monasterboice, a 5th-century monastic site.

Wicklow Mountains

WICKLOW MOUNTAINS, GLENDALOUGH & KILKENNY
Length of trip: 10 hours

Soak in the scenic Wicklow Mountains, as you travel by coach through the area known as the 'garden of Ireland'. You'll also get to enjoy guided walking tours around Glendalough and Kilkenny, visiting sites from films such as Braveheart and P.S I Love You.

BLARNEY CASTLE, ROCK OF CASHEL & CAHIR CASTLE
Length of trip: 12 hours

Head south (through Co. Tipperary and Co. Cork) on this coach trip to discover three of Ireland's major landmarks and cultural sites. On this tour, you'll pay visits to the Rock of Cashel, Cahir Castle and then onto Blarney Castle, to kiss the famous Blarney Stone!

SCAN THE QR CODE'S NEXT TO EACH DESTINATION TO BOOK HIGHLY RATED DAY TRIPS VIA GET YOUR GUIDE.

Giant's Causeway

Cliffs of Moher

Blarney Castle

THE RING OF KERRY

Length of trip: 15 hours

This rail day tour might be an early starter, but if you're wanting to experience the world-renowned Ring of Kerry landscapes, mountains and seascapes, then it's worth the journey! Stop-offs include the Lakes of Killarney, Dingle Bay and Carrauntoohil (Ireland's highest mountain).

CLIFFS OF MOHER & GALWAY

Length of trip: 13 hours

Explore Ireland's west coast, including visits to the iconic Cliffs of Moher, the Burren and Galway. You'll travel via bus (be aware there's up to 2 hours between some stops); however, the travel time is worth it to experience parts of the epic Wild Atlantic Way!

Essential Information A-Z

In this section you'll find all the essential information you'll need to plan your trip to Dublin.

PAGES 230 - 245

ESSENTIAL INFORMATION A-Z
DUBLIN

Accessibility

Accessible destinations, eateries and places to stay are highlighted throughout the entire guide. Look for the 👤 icon. Restrictions may apply, always check directly with the location before visiting.

Public Transport

We've summarised the accessibility aspects of Dublin's public transport below. Use the Transport For Ireland (TFI) Journey Planner to plan accessible routes. Visit transportforireland.ie/accessibility for more information or contact their accessibility officer via email *(accessibility@nationaltransport.ie)*.

Bus
Dublin Bus: Dublin Bus have one wheelchair space that fits standard wheelchairs of up to 70cm wide and 120cm long.
Bus Éireann: Bus Éireann operate a number of buses with entrance ramps and designated wheelchair spaces. Almost 70% of its passenger fleet is accessible. Advance booking is required on inter-city routes.

Rail
Dart: Dart trains feature generous space for wheelchairs, but not every station is wheelchair accessible. Search for your station online via Irish Rail and check its accessibility.
Luas: Luas (Dublin's tram) is compliant with current accessibility and environmental standards for transport systems.

Taxi
Wheelchair accessible taxis are indicated by a wheelchair icon on the roof sign. They have been specifically modified with specialist equipment including ramps, wheelchair anchorages and suitable seatbelts.

Beach Wheelchair Hire

Several of the beaches mentioned within the 'Beyond the City' district (such as Killiney Beach) offer a beach wheelchair hire scheme, although this usually only runs throughout the summer months. Check out *disability-federation.ie* for further details, you'll often need to book hire in advance.

Dog-Friendly Travel

Planning to travel with your dog? Although (as you'll see throughout the guide), there are many eateries, hotels and attractions that are happy to welcome your four-legged friend, getting around the city might come with some issues as there are restrictions on public transport services across Dublin. Visit the *Transport for Ireland (TFI)* website for more information.

Dog-friendly destinations, eateries and places to stay are highlighted

ESSENTIAL INFORMATION A-Z
DUBLIN

throughout the entire guide. Look for the 🐾 icon. Restrictions apply to some destinations, as some have designated areas for your companions and others may require them to be on a lead.

Drugs, Alcohol & Smoking

There are just a few things we thought we'd highlight in relation to drugs, alcohol and smoking in Ireland:

- The possession and use of all drugs (from marijuana to cocaine) is illegal in Ireland.
- It's illegal to be intoxicated (alcohol or drugs) in a public place, although, unless you're causing trouble, you should be fine - so make sure you're behaving yourself!
- You'll need to be 18+ to buy an alcoholic drink from both an off license and from a premises serving alcohol.
- When visiting a pub, children under 15 years of age must be supervised by an adult at all times and they must leave the premises before 9pm (10pm from May to September). There is an exception to the time restriction if children are attending a private function where a meal is being served.
- It's illegal to smoke indoors, so make sure you're taking your cigarette breaks out in the open.

Electricity

Plugs: Type G – three-prong outlet
Electricity: 230v/50Hz

Emergency Numbers

Emergency services (Police/Garda, Ambulance, Fire and Coastal Rescue) – 999 or 112

Store St. Garda (Police) Station, Dublin City Centre - +353 (0) 1 666 8000

Tourist SOS (support for victims of crime) - +353 (0) 1 66 10 562

Rape Crisis Centre (national 24-hour helpline) - +353 1800 778 888

Irish Tourist Assistance Service - +353 (0) 1 666 9354

ESSENTIAL INFORMATION A-Z
DUBLIN

E-Sims

Using an e-SIM is a convenient way to access data on your smart phone without incurring additional fees from your network (easily done). An e-SIM is a built-in digital SIM card activated by scanning a QR code or entering a code and lasting for the duration of your chosen package.

Purchasing an e-SIM at the airport will cost more, so it's better to connect to Wi-Fi and purchase one online. Companies like Maya, Saily, and Revolut offer e-SIM packages.

Language

Generally speaking, you won't need to communicate in any language other than English while visiting Dublin. However, if you want to brush up on your Irish (Gaeilge)—which we believe is a polite gesture when visiting a new country—we've listed some helpful pointers below.

Firstly, a bit about the country's official language: Irish (Gaelic) is primarily spoken in certain areas of rural Ireland known as Gaeltacht regions. Most Irish people you encounter will know a cúpla focal (a few words) of Irish, as it has been a compulsory subject in both primary and secondary schools since 1922. In 2003, the government introduced the Official Languages Act, which mandates that all road signs, street signs, and official documents are displayed in either Irish or both Irish and English. So, keep an eye on those road signs—you might pick up a few phrases!

Oh, and one more thing, an important phrase to remember is **"sláinte!" (meaning "cheers" or "good health"),** which you can use when raising a glass or two!

IRISH SLANG

Craic
Meaning: Fun
"It was great craic"

Grand
Meaning: Good
"That's grand"

Gas
Meaning: Funny
"That's gas"

Class/ Deadly
Meaning: Great/Excellent
"That film was class/deadly"

Cod/Codding You
Meaning: Joking
"Are you codding me"

Banjaxed
Meaning: Broken/ Tired/ Drunk
"I'm banjaxed"

Eejit
Meaning: Idiot/Fool
"What a buck eejit"

Yoke
Meaning: Thing
"Give us that yoke there"

ESSENTIAL INFORMATION A-Z
DUBLIN

COMMON PHRASES

Hello
Dia duit
Pronounced: dee-ah-gwit

Good morning
Maidin mhaith
Pronounced: maw-jin maw-h

Good night
Oíche Mhaith
Pronounced: ee-hah wah

Goodbye (for now)
Slán (go fóill)
Pronounced: slawn (guh foal)

Thank you
Go raibh maith agat
Pronounced: guh rev mah a-gut

Please
Le do thoil
Pronounced: leh duh huh-ill

Yes
Tá
Pronounced: taw

No
Níl
Pronounced: neel

Excuse me
Gabh Mo Leithscéal
Pronounced: go muh lesh-kale

I'm sorry
Tá brón orm
Pronounced: okh, taw brone orr-um

I don't understand
Ní thuigim
Pronounced: nee hig-im

Pleased to meet you
Tá áthas orm bualadh leat
Pronounced: taw aw-huss or-um boo-uh-luh lyat

LGBTQIA+ Travellers

Dublin is said to be one of the safest and friendliest cities in the world for the LGBTQIA+ community. The highpoint of cultural change came in 2015, when Ireland became the first country in the world to vote overwhelmingly in favour of same sex marriage in a referendum.

Today, Dublin has a vibrant LGBTQIA+ scene! As well as some well-established bars and clubs, Dublin plays host to several annual events and celebrations. Dublin Pride Festival (held in June) has become the second-biggest celebration in the city (after St Patrick's Day), a colourful, diverse and empowering extravaganza! Each August, Dublin hosts Ireland's only LGBTQIA+ film festival, GAZE. If visiting in May, it's also worth checking out the International Gay Theatre Festival.

Medical Services

Health Insurance
Always buy travel insurance for your trip – while hopefully it will not be needed – it is essential in a medical emergency.
EU Nationals are entitled to a European Health Insurance Card (EHIC) which can be used for free medical treatment – doctor visits, prescriptions and medical emergencies. It is advisable to apply for a card before travelling to Ireland.

ESSENTIAL INFORMATION A-Z
DUBLIN

Medical Services Continued

General Health
Ordinarily, no vaccinations are required to travel to Ireland*. For minor illnesses, pharmacies can offer valuable advice and provide over-the-counter medication. A note for women: the 'morning after pill' is available to purchase at pharmacies, where you won't need a prescription.

Hospitals, General Practices & Dental Practices
Find information on local hospitals, GP's, dental practices and out of hours services via hse.ie.

*requirements can change, check ahead of travel.

Money

Currency: Euro €
Cash & Cards: Cards are widely accepted, although some eateries may only accept cash. ATMs are widespread. If your bank applies charges for international transactions, we'd suggest creating an account with Revolut, Monzo or Starling to benefit from live exchange rates and no additional charges. You'll need to allow 2-3 weeks before your trip to apply and receive a physical card, or add instantly to your smart phone wallet.

Public Holidays

- New Year's Day (1 January)
- First Monday in February, or 1 February if the date falls on a Friday
- Saint Patrick's Day (17 March)
- Easter Monday
- First Monday in May
- First Monday in June
- First Monday in August
- Last Monday in October
- Christmas Day (25 December)
- Saint Stephen's Day (26 December)

Shops and pubs close on Christmas Day and New Years Day, public transport does not operate on Christmas Day and operates under restricted hours on New Years Day. Opening hours may differ across other public holidays, bear this in mind if travelling to Dublin on a public holiday.

Public Toilets

Unfortunately, there aren't currently any on-street public toilet facilities in Dublin, Dublin City Council have commented that such facilities are too expensive to run. Instead, you'll be able to find public toilet facilities within shopping centres.

Public Transport

Bus: Operates across the county.
LUAS: Dublin's tram service.
DART: Dublin's train system.
Irish Rail: Journey elsewhere in Ireland.
Dublin Bikes: Rent and ride.

ESSENTIAL INFORMATION A-Z
DUBLIN

Safety

Generally speaking, Dublin is a safe city to visit, even if you're travelling solo, but it's wise to take precautions. Here are some tips:
- Keep an eye on your belongings in crowded areas to avoid theft.
- Avoid carrying valuables or large sums of cash; store your passport and cash separately.
- Don't keep all your cash in one place; if traveling with others, divide it among yourselves.
- Use ATMs located in shopping malls or banks instead of those on the street.
- Avoid walking alone after dark, and stick to populated areas.

Tap Water

It's perfectly safe to drink tap water in Dublin. Ireland's water supply undergoes strict treatment and filtration processes to ensure it meets all European and Irish drinking water regulations.

Taxis

Download Uber, Free Now or Bolt, the safest way to order a taxi (plus you'll know before agreeing to the charge how much your journey will cost). You could also download the TFI Driver Check App, this allows you to check that a driver is licensed.

Tourist Information Points

Fáilte Ireland (the National Tourism Development Authority of Ireland) have two tourist information centres in Dublin **(Barnardo Square and O'Connell Street)**. Visit for free and independent advice and information.

Visas*

EU Citizen / European Economic Area: You don't need a visa for tourism if you are a EU citizen or from a country in the European Economic Area (Norway, Iceland and Liechtenstein).
U.S. Citizen: You can enter visa-free for tourism or business stays of up to 90 days.
Short Stay 'C' Visa: Citizens of visa-required countries can apply for a short stay visa for visits up to 90 days.
Short Stay Visa Waiver Programme: This programme allows nationals of certain countries, who have entered the UK on a UK short stay visa, to travel to Ireland without the requirement to obtain an Irish visa. *visa requirements can change, check ahead of travel.*

Weather

Average temperatures in Dublin each season:

Spring 8°C/46°F	Autumn 10°C/50°F
Summer 15°C/59°F	Winter 5°C/41°F

Train & Tram Services Map

238

There's more to Ireland than Dublin...

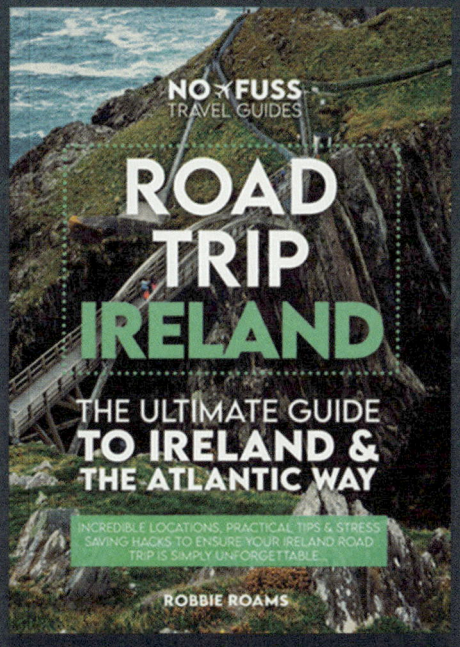

An epic road trip awaits!

Visit nofusstravelguides.com
or scan the QR code to the right

NOTES / JOURNAL

NOTES / JOURNAL

NOTES / JOURNAL

NOTES / JOURNAL

ITINERARY PLANNING

DAY:	
ATTRACTIONS:	**EATERIES:**

DAY:	
ATTRACTIONS:	**EATERIES:**

DAY:	
ATTRACTIONS:	**EATERIES:**

DAY:	
ATTRACTIONS:	**EATERIES:**

ITINERARY PLANNING

DAY:	
ATTRACTIONS:	**EATERIES:**

DAY:	
ATTRACTIONS:	**EATERIES:**

DAY:	
ATTRACTIONS:	**EATERIES:**

DAY:	
ATTRACTIONS:	**EATERIES:**

BUDGET PLANNING

DAY:		
	PLANNED SPEND	**ACTUAL SPEND**
FOOD & DRINK		
TRANSPORT		
ATTRACTIONS		
ACCOMMODATION		
MISC		
TOTAL		

DAY:		
	PLANNED SPEND	**ACTUAL SPEND**
FOOD & DRINK		
TRANSPORT		
ATTRACTIONS		
ACCOMMODATION		
MISC		
TOTAL		

DAY:		
	PLANNED SPEND	**ACTUAL SPEND**
FOOD & DRINK		
TRANSPORT		
ATTRACTIONS		
ACCOMMODATION		
MISC		
TOTAL		

BUDGET PLANNING

DAY:		
	PLANNED SPEND	**ACTUAL SPEND**
FOOD & DRINK		
TRANSPORT		
ATTRACTIONS		
ACCOMMODATION		
MISC		
TOTAL		

DAY:		
	PLANNED SPEND	**ACTUAL SPEND**
FOOD & DRINK		
TRANSPORT		
ATTRACTIONS		
ACCOMMODATION		
MISC		
TOTAL		

DAY:		
	PLANNED SPEND	**ACTUAL SPEND**
FOOD & DRINK		
TRANSPORT		
ATTRACTIONS		
ACCOMMODATION		
MISC		
TOTAL		

Index

PAGES 248 - 253

INDEX
DUBLIN

A
Abbey Theatre 46
Axe Club Dublin 53

B
Bord Gáis Energy Theatre 196

C
Chester Beatty Library 146
Christ Church Cathedral 96
Craic Den Comedy Club 124
Croke Park Stadium & GAA Museum 55
Cycle Dublin Bike & E-Bike Tours 151

D
Dalkey & Dalkey Island 216
DoDublin Bus Tours 47
Dollymount Strand Beach 215
Donabate Beach (Balcarrick Beach) 213
Dublin Bar Academy 74
Dublin Castle 146
Dublin Discovered Boat Tours 192
Dublinia Viking Museum 96
Dublin Literary Pub Crawl 147
Dublin Mountains Hike 217
Dublin Zoo 79
Dún Laoghaire 215

E
EPIC The Irish Emigration Museum 192
Escape Boats 196
Escape Dublin 151

F
Famine Memorial Sculptures 193
Fitzwilliam Square 177
Forty Foot 216

G
Gaiety Theatre 150
Game of Throwing 75
Garden of Remembrance 49
Gate Theatre 48
George's Street Arcade 147
Glasnevin: Ireland's National Cemetery 55
GPO Museum 46
Grand Canal Dock 196
Great South Wall & Poolbeg Lighthouse 197
Guinness Storehouse 101

H
Ha'penny Bridge 122
14 Henrietta Street 52
Howth 213
Hugh Lane Gallery 49

INDEX
DUBLIN

I

Incognito Escape Room 100
Irish Film Institute 123
Irish Museum of Modern Art 104
Irish National War Memorial Park 104
Irish Whiskey Museum 142
Iveagh Gardens 153

J

James Joyce Cultural Centre 49
Jameson Distillery Bow St. 75

K

Killiney Beach 217
Killiney Hill 217
Kilmainham Gaol 104

L

Laughter Lounge 46
Light House Cinema 75

M

Malahide 213
Marsh's Library 97
Merrion Square Park 175
Molly Malone Statue 142
Museum of Literature Ireland 151
Musical Pub Crawl 122

N

National Botanic Gardens 55
National Concert Hall 153
National Gallery of Ireland 174
National Leprechaun Museum 53
National Library of Ireland 174
National Museum of Ireland - Archaeology 175
National Museum of Ireland - Decorative Arts & History 78
National Museum of Ireland - Natural History 175
National Print Museum 177
North Bull Island 215

O

Olympia Theatre 124
O'Reilly Theatre 49
Oscar Wilde House 176

P

Parnell Monument 48
Pearse Lyons Whiskey Distillery 101
Phoenix Park 78
Photo Museum Ireland 123
Portmarnock Beach (Velvet Strand) 213

R

Rafting.ie 79
Richmond Barracks 104
Roe & Co Distillery 101
Royal Hibernian Academy of

INDEX
DUBLIN

Arts 176

S

Samuel Beckett Theatre 142
Sandymount Strand Beach 215
Secret Street Tours 193
Silver Works Jewellery Making 147
Skerries Beaches (North & South) 212
Skyview Tower 75
Skywalk at Croke Park 55
Smock Alley Theatre 124
South Beach Rush 212
St Mary's Abbey 53
St Michan's Church 74
St Patrick's Cathedral 96
St Stephen's Green 150
Surfdock Watersports 197
Sweny's Pharmacy 174

T

Teeling Whiskey Distillery 97
Temple Bar Food Market 124
Temple Bar Gallery & Studios 122
The Academy 46
The Dublin Liberties Distillery 100
The Gravedigger Ghost Bus Tour 146
The Hungry Tree at King's Inns 52
The Irish Rock 'N' Roll Museum Experience 123
The Jeanie Johnston: An Irish Famine Story 192
The Little Museum of Dublin 176
The National Wax Museum Plus 125
The Spire 47
The Stella Cinema Rathmines 153
The Sugar Club 177
The Temple Bar Pub 123
Trinity College & The Book of Kells 142

U

Urban Brewing Tours 192

V

Vicar Street 100
Vico Baths 216
Viking Splash Tours 150
Vintage Tea Trips 150

W

Walking Food Tours 100
Wellington Monument 78
Whelan's Live Music Venue 153
Windmill Lane Studio Tours 197
World of Illusion 125

Our Story

Wondering how No Fuss Travel Guides began? This section will explain.

PAGES 254 - 259

NO FUSS TRAVEL GUIDES
OUR STORY

At No Fuss Travel Guides, we've redefined what a great travel guidebook should look, feel, and read like. Our Amazon best-sellers have been featured in *The Guardian* and *The Sunday Times,* inspiring thousands of epic adventures across the UK, Europe, and the world. Our acclaimed guidebooks cover everything from breathtaking landscapes and must-see destinations to stress-saving tips, eatery recommendations, places to stay, detailed itineraries, and everything in between! But what makes our guides different?

We take a personal approach. Our independent, self-published guidebooks are written in a down-to-earth tone, based on in-depth research and personal, first-hand experiences. Our team of experienced travellers (both human and four-legged) have explored destinations across the UK and beyond, bringing you recommendations that are both authentic and unbiased.

Think of us as your best mate sharing insider travel tips and unforgettable experiences over a pint. We believe in keeping things simple, fun, and informative—helping adventurers plan unforgettable trips with ease and maximise travel time without the stress.